Celebrating the Rites
A PRACTICAL GUIDE

Foundations in Faith®

Bob Duggan • Rita Ferrone
Gael Gensler • Steve Lanza
Donna Steffen

RESOURCES FOR CHRISTIAN LIVING®
Allen, Texas

Nihil Obstat
Rev. Msgr. Glenn D. Gardner, J.C.D.
Censor Librorum

Imprimatur
† Most Rev. Charles V. Grahmann
Bishop of Dallas

August 24, 2001

The Nihil Obstat and Imprimatur are official declarations that the material reviewed is free of doctrinal or moral error. No implication is contained therein that those granting the Nihil Obstat and Imprimatur agree with the contents, opinions, or statements expressed.

Foundations in Faith is registered in U.S. Patent and Trademark Office.

Send all inquiries to:
RCL•Resources for Christian Living
200 East Bethany Drive
Allen, Texas 75002-3804

Toll free   800-822-6701
Fax   800-688-8356

Printed in the United States of America

12728   ISBN 0-7829-0999-X

1 2 3 4 5 6 7 8 9 10

01 02 03 04 05

ACKNOWLEDGMENTS

Excerpts from the English translation of *Rite of Christian Initiation of Adults* ©1985, International Committee on English in the Liturgy, Inc. (ICEL).

The Scripture quotations contained herein are from the New Revised Standard Version Bible: Catholic Edition copyright © 1993 and 1989 by the Division of Christian Education of the National Council of the Churches of Christ in the U.S.A. Used by permission. All rights reserved.

Excerpts from *Vatican Council II, Volume 1, Revised Edition: The Conciliar & Post Conciliar Documents* edited by Austin Flannery, O.P. copyright © 1998, Costello Publishing Company, Inc., Northport, NY are used by permission of the publisher, all rights reserved. No part of these excerpts may be reproduced, stored in a retrieval system, or transmitted in any form or by any means—electronic, mechanical, photo-copying, recording or otherwise, without express permission of Costello Publishing Company.

Excerpts from the *General Directory for Catechesis* Copyright © 1997 United States Catholic Conference, Inc.—Libreria Editrice Vaticana.

Excerpts from the English edition of *Ceremonial of Bishops,* the Liturgical Press, Collegeville, MN, 1989.

Excerpts from *Worship,* January, 1997, pp. 70–71.

Contents

Introduction **5**

PART I
Liturgical Ritual—Essential Understandings **7**

PART II
The Major Rites **15**

   First Step: Acceptance into the Order of Catechumens **16**

   Second Step: Election or Enrollment of Names **31**

      • Rite of Sending **31**

      • Rite of Election **43**

   The Scrutinies **45**

   Third Step: Celebration of the Sacraments of Initiation **59**

   Rite of Reception Outside the Easter Vigil **69**

PART III
The Minor Rites **79**

   Rites Belonging to the Period of the Catechumenate **80**

      • Celebrations of the Word

      • Minor Exorcisms

      • Blessings

      • Anointing with the Oil of Catechumens

   Rites Belonging to the Period of Purification and Enlightenment **82**

      • Presentation of the Creed and the Lord's Prayer

      • Preparation Rites on Holy Saturday

   Rite of Dismissal **92**

Appendix **95**

INTRODUCTION

One of the mantras of those who pioneered the implementation of the *Rite of Christian Initiation of Adults* has been that the RCIA is a process, not a program. Theologian Aidan Kavanagh has reminded us, however, that the RCIA is—first and foremost—a sacramental rite, an act of worship, an official liturgical document that is part of the Roman Ritual of the Catholic Church. In a very real sense, all of our efforts at evangelization and our preaching of conversion, all of the months and years of catechetical activity, all of the pastoral care and spiritual formation lavished on candidates and their sponsors alike, all of the efforts to involve catechumens in apostolic action and the life of the community, all of our strategies to involve the larger parish community in the initiatory experience—all of these—are simply what must be done so that the rites may be celebrated with the sort of "full, conscious and active participation" that Vatican II called for as the birthright of the baptized.

Thus, **Celebrating the Rites** is integrally tied to each of the other volumes in the *Foundations in Faith* series. It would be hard to overstate how crucial is a vibrant liturgical experience for the success of the initiatory process. Nowhere is the authenticity of a Catholic community's faith put to the test so severely as in the liturgical assembly. Students of religion have long noted that Catholics are a sacramental people—that the core of our Catholic identity lies in an appreciation for, a love and a valuing of the sacraments as the heart of our faith. Indeed, the Second Vatican Council has proclaimed that "the liturgy is the summit toward which the activity of the Church is directed; it is also the fount from which all her power flows" (*Constitution on the Sacred Liturgy* 10). We must never lose sight of the fact that the process of Christian initiation is focused unswervingly on introducing candidates and catechumens into the sacramental life of the Church, the liturgical assembly and in particular the eucharistic banquet.

The breathtaking assumption that underlies the *Rite of Christian Initiation of Adults* is that it is precisely in the "full, conscious and active participation" (*Constitution on the Sacred Liturgy* 14) in the liturgical rituals of Christian initiation that one becomes in the fullest sense Catholic. Our deeply held belief in the power of sacraments was expressed by theologians of another era in the Latin dictum that sacraments work *ex opere operato*. What that phrase sought to capture is nothing less than the conviction that the power of the paschal mystery itself is unleashed when the community celebrates in sign and symbol the dying and rising of Jesus Christ. The ancient adage that Christians are "made, not born," referred more to the power of God actively working in the sacraments of the Church than it did to the sweat of catechetical teams laboring to form faith in the clay of inquiring minds and hearts. The audacious claim we Catholics make is that *in the rituals themselves* there is a transforming power at work that carries a person from unbelief to full faith.

Note well: we are not talking about magic ritual here, as if the mere observance of the prescribed cues were sufficient to cause faith to happen. On the contrary, it is the intersection of intentional faith and the hard work of preparing and executing rituals well that results in the effective power of God's grace. Only when divine grace and human initiative conspire to work together do our rituals transform hearts and minds, "making" Christians, and seeing to it—as the language of sacramental theology used to put it—that the celebration of the sacraments is "fruitful." This volume is intended as a tool to help parish communities produce those "fruitful" rituals through which Christians will be well made. Its readership will of course include presiders, worship teams, parish liturgists, and musicians. But equally important is that key members of the catechumenal team—directors, catechists, and others—also understand the vision that is set forth here of what constitutes good liturgical ritual and the steps that must be taken to prepare for and execute celebrations that are engaging, life-giving and ultimately transformative.

PART ONE

Liturgical Ritual—
Essential
Understandings

Liturgical Ritual— Essential Understandings

Understanding Rituals

We humans seem to both love and require rituals for our survival. Developmental psychologists have studied how amazingly early it is that mothers and infants develop bonding and feeding rituals, and the studies of both anthropologists and sociologists have traced the important part that ritual plays in the human community across the life span and in virtually every human culture and society. There is, in fact, an enormous literature available from the social sciences that can help us understand what rituals are and how they work.

But why bother with such information from the scientific community when the *Rite of Christian Initiation of Adults* (RCIA) is a liturgical ritual? Don't sacramental and liturgical theology tell us everything we need to know about how God works in the sacraments of the Church? The answer to those questions can be found in a famous Latin phrase used by Scholastic theologians since the Middle Ages: *gratia supponit naturam.* "Grace builds on nature," the theologians taught, and in so saying they wished to remind us that God's grace deeply respects how our human nature operates. While insisting that the grace of God in the sacraments is always active and its availability does not depend on the holiness of the human minister, traditional Catholic theology also teaches that its effectiveness is very much related to human factors. The "fruitful reception" of the sacraments, in this understanding, is directly related to the dispositions of mind and heart by which a person is more or less open to God's offer of grace. And those dispositions are profoundly influenced by the kind of factors that the social sciences study and report are important for the "success" of a ritual experience.

One of the most basic points to keep in mind about ritual is that its "language" is symbol and symbolic action. Unlike a scientific lecture or the precise, methodical routines that regulate

procedures in a surgery suite, symbols and rituals are evocative and open to many different interpretations. The reason for this is that by their very nature symbols contain a "fullness of meaning" that sets them apart from technical language and mechanical operations. The ring that a young lover gives to his beloved as a symbol of their mutual commitment is rich with meaning on many levels. One might even say that a wedding ring's "meaning" is literally inexhaustible, since the depth of its significance continues to grow across a lifetime of shared experience, sacrifice, joys, and sorrows. Likewise, the action of exchanging rings in the wedding ceremony embodies multiple levels of meaning, both for the bride and groom and for their family and friends who participate in the celebration.

Ritual studies help us to understand how important it is that primary symbols be allowed to "speak" with a primary force in any given ritual action. They also remind us that the very power of a primary symbol can be compromised when it is crowded out with an excess of secondary symbols. A marriage celebration where the couple's exchange of vows and rings is overshadowed by the reading of their favorite love-poetry, the presentation of flowers to mothers, and the release of butterflies as the climactic moment would have to be judged as seriously flawed. Successful rituals are those in which the primary symbols are allowed to speak with full force, and where the overall flow of the ritual action supports and is consistent with the meanings embedded in those primary symbols. This is the reason why liturgists urge so strongly that the symbols used in worship should be lavish, robust and authentic in nature. In Baptism, water must flow in abundance and evoke the ambiguous reality of nature itself, where water brings about both death and life. The sacramental use of oil, another primary sacramental symbol, is compromised if its evocative power is minimized by its being held in a soaked piece of cotton in a tiny container and then applied with the merest touch of the thumb. Oil must be seen and smelled, felt, and experienced as a loving caress when it is applied, or else it is able to connote healing and strengthening only with great difficulty. Grace builds on nature, and the anthropologists remind us that symbols "work" best when they are experienced with the full impact of their primal power.

Rituals are, of necessity, deeply traditional because they embody the inherited values, meanings, categories, and even contradictions contained in a given historical community. In fact, one of the most important social functions of ritual is to transmit vital cultural information and processes from one generation to another. Rituals remind a community of whom they are by preserving ancestral memories that put participants in touch with their history. That is one reason why the power of rituals is tied very closely to repetition and familiarity, rather than to novelty or innovation. The implication of this for liturgical ritual is that those responsible for the choreography of any given rite must be thoroughly familiar with its history and traditional theological meanings. Both the stories of Sacred Scripture in which certain symbols play a prominent part and the accumulated usage of those symbols in religious contexts over many centuries have resulted in a specific history, an identity, that is carried in the symbol itself. The meanings contained in a symbol have been "layered" through the process of its transmission and use that often stretches back to our very beginning as a people. That is why liturgists so frequently cringe at stories of innovations such as butterflies being used in the liturgy to make Easter more "meaningful."

Because the language of symbol and ritual is so multifaceted, rituals also hold the potential of subverting the status quo of a society by generating new, transformative structures and meanings. Anthropologists are fascinated with the way in which ritual functions both to support and to challenge the social body. On the one hand, ritual promotes social cohesion by spelling out what it means to belong to a group, the rules and reigning categories of the society, and so forth. While on the other hand, ritual can also release power for change by evoking new possibilities in the imaginations of those who participate. Rituals can both construct and deconstruct the social fabric of a society. Hence, the power that they exert within a group is enormous. Nathan Mitchell captures a sense of this in the following remarks:

> Rituals do not simply affirm our experience, they rearrange, redescribe, rewrite, redefine it. We emerge from the ritual process different, changed, altered . . . [Rituals] summon us to responses of faith and self-commitment by our very use of them. . . . Ritual is not so much a way of thinking or speaking as it is a technology, an embodied skill that redefines the person who uses it. We become hospitable, for instance, not by analyzing hospitality but by greeting guests,

offering them the kiss of peace, washing their feet, serving them food, adoring Christ's presence in them. For the goal of ritual is not to produce a meaning, but to produce an outcome—a person redefined by grace as God's own welcoming heart and hand. (*Worship*, January 1997, pp. 70 and 71)

Using the Ritual Book

In the article by Nathan Mitchell quoted above, he mentions at one point that rituals "are things to be done, 'scores' for performance . . ." This raises the issue of the importance of learning how to read the "score" that the *Rite of Christian Initiation of Adults* represents in order to "perform" the rituals properly. Just as one needs to know what all of the markings on a musical score mean in order to sight read a piece of music, so the preparation and execution of the various initiatory rites require a background knowledge of the Roman Ritual and the shape it has taken in the post-Vatican II liturgical reform.

One of the characteristic features of the reformed liturgical books issued after the Second Vatican Council is the importance of the introductions (Latin: *praenotanda*) that are placed at the beginning and elsewhere in the rites. These offer an important pastoral and theological context for understanding and celebrating the rituals in question. They also provide essential commentary on the various parts of the rituals, how they "fit" in the overall context of the celebration, and how they are to be implemented and adapted. Adaptations are generally divided into those that are the responsibility of the Episcopal Conference, the local ordinary, and the presider. Knowing whose competency it is to make each of these adaptations can avoid confusion and inappropriate changes. For all of these reasons, it should be clear that one cannot perform intelligently the "score" of any of the catechumenal rituals without an intimate knowledge of the *praenotanda* that are so important a part of the ritual book.

Proper use of the *Rite of Christian Initiation of Adults* also requires an understanding of the different kinds of material contained in any given ritual. The rubrics are like stage directions, and they bear careful reading. They offer practical help orchestrating details of the rite's choreography, and they can frequently give a "feel" for the way a ritual is put together and how parts transition into one another to insure a smooth ritual flow. There are also texts in the rites that are offered by way of example, to give the presider a sense of how his own words should be directed. These need not be slavishly followed verbatim, since they are meant to be suggestive and evocative, not necessarily treated as a script. On the other hand, there are certain prayer texts that are indeed meant to be proclaimed just as written. Most often these texts are of venerable lineage and represent a carefully worked out theology of initiation. To improvise on such texts hardly seems advisable. Sometimes the rite itself offers two or more alternatives for a single prayer, or introduces a segment with the expression "in these or similar words." There are also instances where a ritual action/gesture is optional and may therefore be omitted. Usually this is an indication that the presider may exercise some discretion in adapting what is found in the rite.

In examining the table of contents of the *Rite of Christian Initiation of Adults,* one is struck immediately by the division of the book into two major sections: Part I is the fullest articulation of the catechumenal process for adults, and a case can be made for this being the normative vision of how all Christian initiation is meant to be celebrated in the Catholic Church today. Part II contains derivative and adapted forms of Christian initiation for children of catechetical age, for baptized but uncatechized adults, for initiation in emergency circumstances, and for the reception of baptized Christians from other denominations. In the implementation of the rites in Part II, it is important to keep in mind what is said in Part I, since on occasion there are omissions or inconsistencies in Part II that must be resolved in light of the normative vision of Part I. For example, the rites for use with children seem to presume that young people might be intimidated by public ritual and sometimes fare better with a more minimalist use of symbols. Both of these assumptions deserve to be challenged, and usually the more robust manner of celebration that is suggested in Part I works equally well for children as well as for adults. The edition of the rite currently in use in dioceses of the United States also contains adapted versions of the rites for use with baptized candidates and for when both candidates and catechumens have been included in a single celebration. The success of these adaptations is somewhat uneven, and pastoral flexibility is sometimes required in order to maintain fidelity to the vision of Part I.

Editions of the rite published in the United States have an appendix containing the "National Statutes for the Catechumenate" of the U. S. bishops as well as documentation concerning the catechumenate from the Second Vatican Council and the *Code of Canon Law.* This corpus of legislation is important background reading and can offer practical guidelines for some of the pastoral issues that parish ministers face on a regular basis. It is also worth noting that the edition of the rite published in Canada is somewhat different from that used in the United States. Slight variations in paragraph numbers between the U.S. and Canadian editions also require vigilance when following citations given in articles and commentaries on the rite.

Ritual in the Catechumenal Process

We have noted above that as a part of the Roman Ritual, the *Rite of Christian Initiation of Adults* is primarily a score for liturgical celebration. But it is also a pastoral-theological document that guides a process of evangelization and catechesis. The *Catechism of the Catholic Church* (CCC) and the *General Directory for Catechesis* (GDC), promulgated by Pope John Paul II in 1992 and 1997 respectively, are also foundational documents that give direction to the ministry of the Word through the Church's efforts at evangelization and catechesis. Especially in the *General Directory for Catechesis* and in the *Rite of Christian Initiation of Adults,* the vital role of liturgical celebrations in the process of faith formation is made abundantly clear. This is consistent with what we know from the social sciences about how rituals shape consciousness, form values, and instill core identity. But these modern sources are only reminding us of what the Church has known from its earliest beginnings: that when we gather for worship in the power of the Holy Spirit, Christian consciousness and faith are formed and shaped in a privileged fashion. In fact, earlier centuries referred to the liturgy as the "school of faith."

This way of thinking is quite different from the approach that has dominated western approaches to education and catechetical theory in modern times, and we should be very attentive to the "new" direction that the Church is indicating for us in these documents. In the context of the catechumenal process, it is clear that the liturgical celebrations themselves are meant to have a primary role in forming (and informing) the faith journey of candidates and catechumens. The rites are not mere window dressing, nor are they optional elements that simply mark progress already made. In a very real way, each celebration is meant to carry forward the catechumenal journey of those who celebrate them. The major transitional rituals, in particular, can be thought of as "rites of passage," rituals that not only signify but, in fact, effect a change of status and identity in the Christian community. Something decisive happens to an inquirer at the "Rite of Acceptance," so much so that those who have passed through that doorway are, in the words of the *Decree on the Church's Missionary Activity,* "already joined to the Church, they are already of the household of Christ" (14). Similarly, the "Rite of Election" and the sacraments of initiation celebrated at the Easter Vigil profoundly change the very identity of those who celebrate them. A subtle but significant cue regarding the importance ascribed to the catechumenal liturgies is found in a rubric regarding the celebration of the scrutinies. So significant are these rites for the lenten transformation of the elect, that in order for someone to miss even one of them, the specific permission of the local bishop must be sought. And the bishop, in turn, is directed to grant such permission only "on the basis of some serious obstacle, from one scrutiny or, in extraordinary circumstances, even from two" (RCIA 34.3; cf. 331).

A careful examination of how the rituals in the *Rite of Christian Initiation of Adults* are positioned in the overall catechumenal process will show that there is a very definite developmental plan presumed by the ritual structure. The understanding of conversion embodied in the rite involves a process that is gradual and developmental. Thus, the rites themselves only ask for (and celebrate) the level of conversion that is appropriate at each and every stage of the journey. An important implication of this fact is the need for careful discernment of readiness prior to each of the rituals. If key transitional rites are calibrated for a specific stage of readiness, then it is important that they be celebrated neither too soon nor too late. This is yet another reason why the "one size fits all" mentality that governs an academic year catechumenal model is irremediably flawed. Not everyone in an inquiry group will be ready to make the promise required in the "Candidates' First Acceptance of the Gospel" (RCIA 52) in the month of October! If we are to take seriously the words and actions of our rites, then those rituals that mark a specific step in the conversion journey must be celebrated in ways that correspond to the truth of the spiritual journey of each and every person who celebrates them.

A renewed appreciation for the importance of liturgical ritual in the process of faith formation has focused attention on what is currently being termed ritual (or liturgical) catechesis. Liturgical catechesis is referred to in the *General Directory for Catechesis* as an "eminent kind of catechesis" (GDC 71) and it is described in the following words: "Liturgical catechesis, prepares for the sacraments by promoting a deeper understanding and experience of the liturgy. This explains the contents of the prayers, the meaning of the signs and gestures, educates to active participation, contemplation and silence" (GDC 71). In the context of the Christian initiation of children, the *General Directory for Catechesis* also describes liturgical catechesis as a "privileged means" of inculturating the faith (GDC 207).

Liturgical catechesis understands that all catechetical activity is, in a real sense, an effort to prepare a person to celebrate the liturgy with that "full, conscious and active participation" (*Constitution on the Sacred Liturgy* 14) that the Second Vatican Council has made the litmus test of authentic spiritual renewal. But liturgical catechesis is not limited to preparing a person to celebrate a particular ritual. It also includes all forms of mystagogy, all those catechetical efforts that aim to unpack the meanings of a ritual once it has been celebrated. Mystagogy is asking (and answering) the question "So what?" What are the implications of participation in a given ritual for the rest of an individual's life? Mystagogy attends in a particular way to the actual ritual experience itself. It looks at the tracing of the cross on the senses, and asks, "Now, how must you live differently in light of that sacred sign that has been impressed upon your very flesh?" It examines the healing and strengthening touch experienced in the scrutinies, and it asks, "How have you been changed by that moment of grace, by the naming of evils, by the power of the community's prayer and the word of Christ pronounced by the priest?" And after the Vigil, "How must you now live differently in the world, given the water bath and anointing you have received with sacred chrism?" Indeed, perceptive catechists are coming to realize that the ongoing catechesis for adult Catholics that is referred to in the *General Directory for Catechesis* as "post-baptismal catechesis" (GDC 91) is in some ways simply a matter of mystagogy, an unfolding of the implications of a Christian's regular participation in the Eucharist.

Celebrating the Rites

One of the favorite metaphors for the process of initiation among the ancient Fathers of the Church was that of a mother giving birth to a child. The mother, in their usage, was the entire community of the Church. That sense of the communal nature of the initiatory process has been recaptured in a powerful way in the contemporary *Rite of Christian Initiation of Adults*. Throughout the ritual book, there is a sustained effort to spell out the various ways that different ministries cooperate in the catechumenal effort. Not surprisingly, those same ministries appear in various ways in the different rituals that are part of the initiatory process.

The foundational liturgical ministry, of course, belongs to the worshiping community as a whole. The rites are all designed as communal celebrations, and the primacy of the Sunday assembly is unmistakable. One practical implication of this theological position is that catechumenal teams need to be deliberate in developing the ways that communities are prepared for and supported in exercising their role. Careful attention has to be devoted to communicating an understanding of the rites to parishioners at large; and, whenever a rite is celebrated, the community must be thoroughly familiar with its parts. In arranging the choreography of a rite, attention must be given to how best to engage the larger assembly in the ritual action as active participants rather than as mere spectators.

The planning and preparation of catechumenal liturgies will require the involvement of various specific liturgical ministries, and it is important that the catechumenal team work to insure a collaborative effort among the many segments of parish life that are involved. Frequently this will mean that special consideration needs to be given to the preparation of ushers, greeters, liturgical artists and others who care for the environment of the worship space, lectors, cantors, accompanists and other musicians, as well as catechists, presiders, homilists, sponsors, parents, godparents, and so forth. The *praenotanda* of the rite encourage that "whenever possible, [catechists should] have an active part in the rites" (RCIA 16). Since the rubrics almost never indicate how this is to be achieved, there remains the opportunity for sensitive liturgical adaptation that will ritualize the important role that catechists play in the process of initiation.

Music is one of the most important factors in achieving the ideal of fully participative liturgical celebrations. There is a growing body of music written specifically for the rites that are part of the catechumenal process; but the repertoire remains rather limited, and continuing efforts are still needed for the full integration of music into the rites. Acclamations, litanies and responses of various sorts provide ample opportunity for the assembly at large to participate musically in the ritual action. More specialized musical creativity is possible and needed for choirs, the presider's sung proclamation of certain texts, and the interaction of cantor and assembly. A good sense of timing and an understanding of the flow of a particular ritual will also help musicians to recognize where the judicious use of hymnody would be appropriate.

What is crucial for the successful use of music in these rites (as in any ritual, in fact) is an understanding that liturgy is musical by nature. Music is not something we add on to the liturgy to dress it up a bit. Rather, the Christian community worships in song as an integral way in which it celebrates the mysteries of salvation. Because music is an art form, success in using it requires technical mastery and a certain level of musicianship. Yet success in liturgical music requires much more than mere technical proficiency. Music that both supports and enhances worship blends the interaction of assembly, soloists, instrumentalists, and choir into a harmonious unity, where each one does no more and no less than is appropriate. The liturgical musician can sometimes achieve true art with the simplest—but absolutely "on target"—use of song to carry forward, punctuate, highlight, or support a given ritual action. Knowing just how to underscore lightly a spoken text, or when to have a cantor sing and the assembly echo a simple refrain; selecting just the right form for a sung litany that will allow processional movement, or focusing the deep meaning of a ritual action with a staccato

acclamation shared by assembly and choir together—these are the ways that the art of liturgical music blends ritual action and communal song into a powerfully engaging experience of liturgical celebration.

What liturgical documents call the "pastoral judgment" in the selection of liturgical music is an amalgam of many different elements. Sensitivity to cultural factors, the ownership that the local assembly has for a particular piece of music, limitations of repertoire and musicians' skill level, a sense of proper timing within the flow of the ritual action, these are just some of the subtle but extremely important factors brought together in the final judgment about how music should be used at any point in a given rite.

Adapting the Rites

It was indicated above that the *praenotanda* of the *Rite of Christian Initiation of Adults* contain indications as to the nature and competencies of specific adaptations to be made by conferences of bishops, the local ordinary, and the minister who presides at a given rite. Sometimes there are also indications within the rubrics of a rite itself about the need for the minister to adapt to the pastoral situation of the participants. Unlike so many other liturgical rituals whose language is one of caution and warning not to tamper with the text, the *Rite of Christian Initiation of Adults* breathes an entirely different spirit, encouraging the making of needed adaptations:

> Celebrants should make full and intelligent use of the freedom given to them. . . . In many places the manner of acting or praying is intentionally left undetermined or two alternatives are offered, so that ministers, according to their prudent pastoral judgment, may accommodate the rite to the circumstances of the candidates and others who are present. In all the rites the greatest freedom is left in the invitations and instructions, and the intercessions may always be shortened, changed or even expanded with new intentions, in order to fit the circumstances or special situations of the candidates. . . . (RCIA 35).

Aside from the development of rituals for use with baptized candidates, virtually nothing has been done thus far in the United States officially to adapt the rite along cultural lines. Pastoral experiments with specific adaptations have been modest to date, and these have been mostly unofficial and local. Genuine liturgical inculturation has simply not yet been attempted.

Nonetheless, the number of initiates who come from distinctive ethnic and cultural groups today constitute a growing challenge to pastoral/liturgical resourcefulness and creativity. It will be up to pastoral ministers at the grass roots level to discover how best to incorporate symbols and rituals of initiation indigenous to a specific people into the larger framework of the rite.

In accommodating any ritual to the local pastoral situation, let alone making more substantive accommodations in the name of inculturation, it is exceedingly important that a community's decisions be thoughtful and wise. One must understand the history and theology of the rite in question, where it fits in the overall pattern of Christian initiation, and the ritual flow that is suggested in the "score" of the rite at a given point. Intelligent adaptation requires an intimate knowledge of the assembly that will celebrate the ritual—their gifts and limitations, their language and customs, their collective story and the immediate context in which they will gather for a particular celebration. Adaptation must always be in the service of a richer celebration of faith, never done for the sake of mere novelty. Prudent creativity is not about "just adding stuff" to make a ceremony more "relevant." It requires knowledge of what is primary in a ritual—its main message and its most important symbols and gestures. One helpful criterion of the wisdom of any proposed adaptation is to ask whether it enhances and allows the primary symbols to speak more clearly, or if it distracts from, overshadows, or obscures what is most important.

The sections of this book offer assistance to those responsible for the implementation of the *Rite of Christian Initiation of Adults* at the local level. Background information and suggestions about how to celebrate the rituals are provided in order to help local communities arrive at their own decisions more thoughtfully and with some measure of creativity. To follow slavishly every idea that is presented in this volume would be just as much a mistake as to take the rite itself and simply follow its script mindlessly, without regard for its effectiveness in one's own community. Those responsible for the liturgies of Christian initiation must keep uppermost in their minds what has been said above about how rituals "work" best, and how we must respect the human needs of those who celebrate in order to promote a "fruitful reception" of the sacraments.

PART TWO

The Major Rites

✧ First Step: Acceptance into the Order of Catechumens

✧ Second Step: Election or Enrollment of Names

✧ The Scrutinies

✧ Third Step: Celebration of the Sacraments of Initiation

✧ Rite of Reception Outside the Easter Vigil

First Step: Acceptance into the Order of Catechumens

The Rite at a Glance

AT THE THRESHOLD . . .
RECEIVING THE CANDIDATES

Greeting

Opening Dialogue

Candidates' First Acceptance of the Gospel

Affirmation by the Sponsors and the Assembly

Signing of the Candidates with the Cross
- Signing of the Forehead
- [Signing of the Senses]
- Concluding Prayer

Invitation to the Celebration of the Word of God

INSIDE THE CHURCH . . .
LITURGY OF THE WORD

Instruction

Readings

Homily

[Presentation of a Bible]

Intercessions for the Catechumens

Prayer over the Catechumens

Dismissal of the Catechumens

THE LITURGY CONTINUES . . .
LITURGY OF THE EUCHARIST

Understanding the Rite

In this, the first public ritual of the *Rite of Christian Initiation of Adults,* a change of identity takes place: inquirers become catechumens. They are welcomed by the Church and signed with the cross of Christ to signify their new status as disciples and members of the household of faith. The ritual text calls this rite the "first consecration" (RCIA 41) of those in the process of initiation, suggesting that in this ritual they are specially marked as God's own by the community of faith.

The **community** and its welcome, along with the **catechumens** and their promise of discipleship are therefore crucial symbols in the rite. Two especially prominent symbols that further define the rite are the **cross,** with which the catechumens are signed, and the **Word,** which is proclaimed, preached, and presented to them. Signing with the cross is an ancient gesture of entry into the catechumenate that has persisted through the centuries in a shortened form as part of the ritual of Baptism. Here it appears in its fullest form, however, and the significance of being marked by the cross of Christ is expanded by the signing of the senses. A ritual presentation of the Scriptures is a modern innovation in this rite, but in a certain sense it too rests on an ancient precedent, since catechumens in the ancient church were those permitted to "hear the Word."

Of great importance to this **threshold** rite is the physical space in which the ritual takes place. The movement *from outside to inside* makes for a strong experience of the spiritual change that is being effected. Ideally, those who will become catechumens are waiting outdoors with their sponsors, and the assembly comes to meet them and bring them in. A keynote of the rite is **welcome,** and this welcome must be expressed by the whole community by the community's full participation. An unfortunate adaptation that is sometimes made in this rite is to have the inquirers knock on the door to gain admittance. A much better sign of the true meaning of this threshold moment is found in having the assembly go out to meet them in joyful welcome.

This rite is also an eloquent expression of the call to **discipleship,** for the newcomer is being invited into a way of life that is patterned on the Gospel. The idea of free choice and **commitment** is found in the rite, especially in the "Candidates' First Acceptance of the Gospel," yet there is also the frequent acknowledgment of unmerited favor or **grace** throughout the prayer texts.

The rite begins with a **dialogue,** which reflects the movement of the precatechumenate. "What is your name and what are you looking for?" are the basic questions that are answered in this exchange. The dialogue leads to the **candidate's First Acceptance of the Gospel,** which is not the passing on of a book, but the embrace of a way of life patterned on the Good News. The importance of the "Candidates' First Acceptance of the Gospel" stems from it being the principal expression by the inquirer that he or she does indeed wish to embrace a life of discipleship. The sponsors and assembly affirm this action and a prayer sums up the exchange. As a sign of their new way of life, the inquirers are then **signed with the cross,** not only on the forehead, but on all their senses and their hands and feet as well. If a cross will be given, it is presented at this time; but the primary liturgical action is the tracing of the cross on the candidates, signifying the involvement of the whole person in the new identity of a disciple. From this point onward, those who have been marked with the cross are to be called "catechumens" (see RCIA 55B).

All then go into the church in procession to take part in the **Liturgy of the Word.** This is the second main portion of the rite. The Word is proclaimed and preached in such a way that it speaks to both the catechumens and the assembly, and unfolds the meaning of what has taken place earlier in the rite. The Scriptures will guide the spiritual journey of the catechumens from this time onward, and so the catechumens are lovingly **presented with the gospels** in some form (a Bible to keep, or reverencing the gospel book or lectionary). The community then prays for them in a litany of **intercession,** which may also include the general intercessions for that Mass, and concludes with a solemn **Prayer Over the Catechumens** with hands extended.

Last of all, the catechumens are **dismissed.** The dismissal shows that their formation in the Word has begun. The assembly is sending them to undertake the work of delving more deeply into what they have heard in the Scriptures. Furthermore, the "Rite of Dismissal" signifies that the catechumenate period is an "in-between" time. The catechumens are now members of "the household of Christ" (RCIA 47), but they are not yet full members who partake of the Eucharist.

Baptized Candidates: What's Different?

In the **combined rite** (RCIA 505 ff), the baptized candidates do everything the unbaptized do, but they are distinguished by the words that are used and by their physical placement (two groups should be visible: the baptized and the unbaptized). When the baptized candidates are introduced, reference is made to their Baptism. They are signed with the cross *as a reminder* of their Baptism, and so on. They are called *candidates* and never *catechumens.* The repetition of every action in the combined rite can be cumbersome (as in the signing of the senses), and judicious choices need to be made in order to keep clear distinctions yet avoid wordiness.

There is also a rite **for candidates only** (RCIA 411 ff) called the "Rite of Welcoming the Candidates." If the rite for candidates alone is used, the candidates *do not gather outside or at the doors of the church* to be welcomed. The candidates begin the liturgy inside the church, in the midst of the faithful. Great freedom for personal witnessing is given in the dialogue described in RCIA 419B.

What About Children?

The rite adapted for children has made only very minor adjustments to the adult ritual. Acknowledgment is made that it is usually the parents, not sponsors, who present the children to the community. The parents are asked to give their consent to the request of the children for Baptism. In addition, the language used throughout has been made simpler and more direct. Most significant appears to be the omission of the "Candidates' First Acceptance of the Gospel," although a careful reading of the rubrics at the end of the opening dialogue (RCIA 264) reveals that the celebrant is invited to ask the children to make a "sign of their assent" in some form. Given the importance of this element in the adult rite, it seems advisable for the celebrant to include this option, asking for a response on the part of the children that is equivalent to the adults' "Candidates' First Acceptance of the Gospel."

Can the rite adapted for children be combined with the adult rite? Certainly. In fact it is very desirable for adults and children to celebrate together, especially in those cases when an entire family is seeking initiation.

Discernment Before the Rite of Acceptance

Discernment is necessary before celebrating the "Rite of Acceptance" for catechumens or the "Rite of Welcoming" for candidates. Hopefully it has already been communicated to inquirers from the time of the first meeting or interview, and by language throughout the precatechumenate, that the amount of time in the precatechumenate will vary from person to person. The *Rite of Christian Initiation of Adults* suggests signs of readiness to be in place before celebrating this rite (RCIA 36, 42). The person is to:

   ✧ desire to change.
   ✧ feel called away from sin.
   ✧ be drawn into the mystery of God's love.
   ✧ have a beginning faith.
   ✧ want to enter into a relationship with God in Christ.
   ✧ have a sense of Church.

Guideposts

Some particular guideposts can be "listened for" during the precatechumenate meetings.

   ✧ Inquirers who are experiencing the beginnings of conversion will offer examples of how they are different. Perhaps they are feeling drawn to reconcile with someone after a lengthy period of time. They may share that they are more patient or compassionate with some family members or coworkers. Inquirers will also frequently express their need and desire to change even more.

   ✧ Along with this, inquirers may state that their relationship with God is becoming more central in their life. They find they are praying more in the morning or evening, or going to or from work. God often becomes a closer friend or companion.

   ✧ Inquirers ready to celebrate this rite will continue to feel drawn to the Catholic community. They experience a sense of community and welcome, find this community a place where they observe the Good News being lived, or see an alive faith that operates in people they know.

   ✧ Central to these examples is that the person finds himself or herself drawn to Christ and to Christ's teaching.

For Unbaptized and Baptized

The signs of readiness already mentioned apply to both the unbaptized and baptized who need a fuller period of formation. Be aware that inquirers may need to wrestle with the family implications of embracing Catholicism. Those who are baptized in another Christian tradition may have particular questions about Catholicism in areas where beliefs differ from their former tradition.

Those Not Ready for the Rite

Discernment is not about judging who is good enough and who is not. Rather it is about naming the truth before God of what is actually happening within the person. Pastorally, what are the deeper needs of the person? What would God want to be said or done to help this person come to a fuller experience of God, of life, and of the Church? Pastoral ministers are tempted to be nice, kind, and move everyone along. Pastorally, doing what is easiest does not benefit the person. Team members usually have a sense of who seems ready and who does not. Listen to this truth. Name what the concerns are. Particular behaviors may be indications that the conversion or change has not occurred. Be aware of these concerns.

   ✧ Arriving late, nonattendance, or nonparticipation may show a lack of personal commitment, or may be evidence of a difficult family or work situation.

   ✧ Continual challenges to the team; repeatedly bringing up all the areas of the Church's shortcomings; or deep anger at God, team members, or others may indicate time is needed to talk about and work with these feelings.

   ✧ Talking only about knowledge with an avoidance of how it relates to the person's real self keeps the faith journey at a distance.

   ✧ Particular family or work situations may be taking precedence in the person's energy and time.

   ✧ Shallow motives of pleasing someone or benefitting one's business may be operating.

   ✧ More time is needed simply because the person has had little acquaintance with faith.

In bringing any concern to the person it is helpful to state the behavior that is noticed and ask the person to talk about their experience. Through this conversation, a deeper understanding of what is operating inside may emerge. At times, change occurs during the conversation. Talking about the concern together can bring about an honest and trusting relationship.

Communication Between Team Members

Those leading the precatechumenate sessions listen for concrete indications of the initial conversion or nonreadiness within the inquirer. When several inquirers have been expressing how they are changing and their desire for Christ and Church, this information is shared with the coordinator. Then individual interviews are held—before a date is communicated to the inquirers. Even when the team feels quite clear that a person is ready to celebrate the "Rite of Acceptance" or the "Rite of Welcoming," having a one-to-one conversation serves the inquirer by helping to name what has been happening inside.

Individual Interviews

The coordinator, pastor, or other team member (whoever has the best skills for this) sets up an appointment of at least 45 minutes with each individual inquirer to talk about what has been happening for them in the precatechumenate.

Discernment Reflection Areas

✧ During the period of inquiry, what changes have you noted in yourself, in your relationship with your family members, and at work?

✧ How would you describe who God is for you now? In what ways has your prayer shifted?

✧ What in you still needs to change? What is your growing edge?

✧ What draws you to be part of this parish community?

✧ What questions of yours are still unanswered?

✧ What circumstances will affect your ability or willingness to continue in the process?

✧ Include here any concerns about an annulment.

✧ Present concerns by the team and ask the inquirer to talk about his or her experience relevant to these concerns.

Team Discernment

After the individual interviews, the coordinator and precatechumenate team gathers. In a context of prayer, listening for God's action in the person and naming this in truth, a determination about the readiness of the inquirer to move to the catechumenate is made. Communication with the inquirer continues.

Scheduling the Rite of Acceptance

Some parishes have two or three fixed times when the "Rite of Acceptance" or the "Rite of Welcoming" is scheduled. Times might include Ordinary Time between Christmas and Lent, Ordinary Time in the early or midsummer, and Ordinary Time in the fall. The Rite also talks about celebrating this step during the Easter season (see RCIA, NS 6). Other parishes wait until several inquirers are ready to celebrate the "Rite of Acceptance" or the "Rite of Welcoming," and then set the date (RCIA 18). Generally the "Rite of Acceptance" or the "Rite of Welcoming" is celebrated at a parish Sunday Mass. In either case, take into consideration:

✧ the liturgical calendar and particular Sunday readings that lend themselves to this rite. Usually the "Rite of Acceptance" or the "Rite of Welcoming" is not celebrated on a feast or in a particular season, such as Advent, when the focus is clearly elsewhere.

✧ the parish calendar. (Do not celebrate this rite when there are Baptisms at Mass, or elongated announcements for events such as a mission, fund-raising, parish council elections.)

✧ the pastor's calendar. Check the pastor's (or associate pastor's) availability.

✧ times when the parish can gather after Mass with refreshments to welcome those who celebrate this rite.

✧ celebrating this rite at various Mass times to involve more of the parish community in initiating new members.

✧ the possibility of celebrating the "Rite of Acceptance" at one Mass and the "Rite of Welcoming" at another Mass when there are both unbaptized and baptized ready for this step.

Spiritual Preparation for the Rite of Acceptance

Gathering

1. Prepare the environment beforehand with a circle of chairs around a table upon which is placed a cloth, a lighted candle, and an open Bible.
2. Have the inquirers sit next to their sponsors.
3. Invite everyone to use a color (or animal or word) to express how they are as they gather.
4. Provide copies of Psalm 27:4–6 and have everyone pray these psalm verses together.

Reflection

1. Give this introduction. *In a moment we will hear of a time when Jesus encountered some disciples. Picture the dry land of Israel, a clear and sunny day, John and two disciples, and Jesus walking by. Let yourself also be there as Jesus walks by.* Then have a team member proclaim John 1:35–39.
2. Give everyone a sheet of paper and a pencil. Have two columns on the paper with the headings *What I want from God is:* and *The Church can assist me in receiving this by.* State: *In the reading, Jesus asks the disciples what they want, what they are looking for. Hear Jesus asking you these same questions.* Invite the participants to write any response that comes to mind. Play reflective music in the background while they are writing. (10–15 minutes)
3. Invite inquirers and sponsors to share with each other what they have written. (15 minutes)
4. Make the following points to the participants:
   - ✧ The Christian journey involves many riches, joys, and blessings.
   - ✧ Christ, however, is the crucified one.
   - ✧ Living as a follower of Jesus involves embracing one's own cross in Christ.
5. Ask participants to reflect for a few moments on the cross they are carrying at this moment on their faith journey. Then have the sponsor-inquirer pairs share their responses.
6. In the total group invite the participants to state in a concise way something about the crosses they are now embracing.

Prayer

End by singing "I Say 'Yes,' My Lord" (Peña, GIA Publications) or another familiar hymn about discipleship.

Announcements

1. Invite the participants to spend a few moments each day in prayer before the "Rite of Acceptance." As a focus they can both speak to God about what they are looking for and what they need as they embrace the cross.
2. Give input about when and where to gather for the "Rite of Acceptance." Tell sponsors when their rehearsal will be. Explain that inquirers will not rehearse but will be guided by their sponsors throughout the rite.

Spiritual Preparation for the Rite of Welcoming

Gathering

1. Prepare a circle of chairs in the area of your church that is used for Baptism. Welcome the participants. Have sponsor-candidate pairs sit together near the font.
2. Ask participants to look at the font. Pray a prayer in your own words asking God to deepen and bring into fullness the Baptism of these men, women, and children.

Reflection

1. Have a team member proclaim Matthew 3:12–18.
2. Invite everyone to listen to the reading again for a word or phrase that strikes them. Proclaim Matthew 3:12–18 again. Invite participants to say the word or phrase aloud.
3. State the following: *By Baptism we too are God's beloved son or daughter. God's favor rests on us.* Then invite: *What is it like to know that you are God's beloved? What does it mean for your life that you are God's beloved?* Have them share their response in sponsor-candidate pairs. Then, invite some sharing in the total group.
4. Ask participants to reflect and share in their sponsor-candidate pairs responses to these questions: *What more do you want in living your Baptism? How can this Church community assist you?* Allow about 15 minutes. Then invite participants to share some of their hopes with everyone.
5. Make the following points:
   - ✧ The Christian journey involves many riches, joys, and blessings.
   - ✧ Christ, however, is the crucified one.
   - ✧ Living as a baptized follower of Jesus involves embracing one's own cross in Christ.
6. Ask participants to reflect for a few moments on the cross they are carrying at this moment on their faith journey. Then have the sponsor-candidate pairs share their responses.
7. In the total group invite the participants to state in a concise way something about the cross they are now embracing.

Prayer

1. Invite sponsors and candidates to come up in pairs to the baptismal font. Have the sponsors take some water and bless the candidates on their foreheads and hands with the holy water.
2. Sing "Gather Your People" (Hurd, OCP) or another familiar hymn about discipleship and Baptism.

Announcements

1. Invite the participants to spend a few moments each day in prayer before the "Rite of Welcoming." As a focus they can both speak to God about what they are looking for and what they need as they embrace the cross.
2. Give input about when and where to gather for the "Rite of Welcoming." Tell sponsors when their rehearsal will be. Explain that inquirers will not rehearse but will be guided by their sponsors throughout the rite.

Catechetical and Spiritual Preparation of Inquirers

Parish sponsors need to be paired up with inquirers before the "Rite of Acceptance" and "The Rite of Welcoming." Sponsors participate in the preparation for the rite with the inquirers. Prior to these gatherings the discernment is made with the inquirers about their readiness for this rite. Inquirers are also informed that beginning with this rite and each Sunday afterward they will participate in the Liturgy of the Word at Sunday Mass and be sent forth, or dismissed, to further reflect on God's Word.

Initial Gathering of Those Preparing for the Rite and Any New Sponsors

Normally inquirers would become acquainted with potential sponsors during the precatechumenate, as parishioners welcome them and share their stories during this time of evangelization. In cases where a sponsor is only matched up with an inquirer at the end of the precatechumenate, a gathering such as the following may be helpful.

Gathering

1. Introduce inquirers to their sponsors as they arrive if this has not already happened.
2. Pray a prayer in your own words, thanking God for bringing all together, for providing companions for the journey of faith, and asking God's blessing on this gathering.

Reflection

1. Give time for each sponsor-inquirer pair to share with each other basic information: name, residence, family members, and work situation. (10 minutes)

2. In pairs, further the sharing. Ask sponsors to tell the inquirers what drew them to be sponsors. Have the inquirer also speak about any previous religious background and what drew them to begin this process of looking at the Catholic faith. (10 minutes)
3. Also in pairs, have the sponsors tell one thing that is important to them about being a Catholic. Have the inquirers share something from the precatechumenate they have come to know about God or Jesus that has been significant for them. (10 minutes)
4. Gather together as a group and do introductions in the larger group. Have each inquirer introduce the sponsor, and each sponsor introduce the inquirer. (10 minutes)
5. Invite participants to share in the large group a word or phrase that describes how they are feeling about this gathering.

Prayer

1. Conclude by proclaiming Colossians 3:12–17.
2. Pray a prayer in your own words.

Announcements

Give directions about the time and place of the next gathering.

Preparing the Ministers

Sponsors

A sponsor accompanies each catechumen and candidate through his or her initiation journey. Sponsors receive some training and background in their role of being a sponsor. See the *Director's Manual* and the *Handbook for Sponsors* from the *Foundations in Faith* series for assistance in sponsor formation.

The formal role of sponsor begins with the "Rite of Acceptance" or "Rite of Welcoming." Sometimes the sponsor is the one who literally introduced the person to the parish community and participates with the inquirer from the beginning. Alternatively the sponsor is paired up with the inquirer during the precatechumenate or when the inquirer is ready to celebrate this rite. In either case, sponsors participate in the preparation for the rite with the inquirer they accompany. (See above.)

Sponsors participate in a rehearsal for the "Rite of Acceptance" or "Rite of Welcoming." Some things they will need to know about their role in this rite are:

❖ Sponsors gather with the person and with other sponsors, catechumens, and candidates when arriving on the day of the rite. The sponsor then takes the catechumen or candidate to the place where they will await the community's welcome.

- ❖ The sponsor physically supports and maintains contact with the person by keeping a hand on the person's shoulder or arm throughout the rite.
- ❖ When the presider invites the introductions, each sponsor introduces himself or herself and the person sponsored to the community, and give some brief information about the person.
- ❖ When signing the catechumens or candidates with the cross, the sponsor actually touches the person and signs the part of the body as it is named, using the entire hand. It is helpful for sponsors to practice this signing with one another at the rehearsal.
- ❖ Sponsors sit with the catechumens and candidates.
- ❖ Each sponsor knows where the catechumen or candidate stands for the presentation of the Word and for the intercessions, and leads him or her there, while keeping a hand on his or her arm or shoulder.
- ❖ At the time of dismissal, sponsors stay in the church for the remainder of Mass.
- ❖ After Mass, sponsors meet with the catechumen or candidate, and introduce him or her to others in the parish at the reception.

Presider

During the weeks before the "Rite of Acceptance" or "Rite of Welcoming" the presider meets with the candidates and the sponsors. This could happen by participating in some of the precatechumenate or preparation sessions, or through being present at social times before or after the sessions. Before the rehearsal for the "Rite of Acceptance" or "Rite of Welcoming" the presider is given the text for the rite, with the names of the baptized, unbaptized, and sponsors. Options in the rite, and placement of people in the worship space are discussed before the rehearsal. The liturgist, coordinator, or presider leads the rehearsal with the sponsors. After walking through the rite any further adaptations or directions may be inserted into the text.

Coordinator

The coordinator knows all the people involved in the rite. The coordinator is at the rehearsal and shares pertinent information. On the day of the rite, the coordinator gathers with the sponsors, catechumens, and candidates, and possibly leads them in a prayer or centering moment of reflection. The coordinator then tells the sponsors to move with the catechumens or candidates to the place where the assembly will welcome them. The coordinator goes to his or her place in the worship space. After the presider's invitation, the coordinator ordinarily addresses the entire assembly stating that those who have been journeying in the time of the precatechumenate

now stand awaiting the welcome of the community. The presider then invites the assembly to follow the cross with him and the coordinator and to surround the catechumens and candidates. The coordinator then may take on various speaking parts in the rite. The coordinator or a catechist will lead the catechumens out after the intercessions and reflect with them on their experience of the rite. (See "Mystagogy," page 29.) When the Mass is over, the coordinator sees to it that the catechumens and candidates are taken to the reception.

Cantor

The cantor is extremely important in bringing the entire assembly into the celebration of the rite. Ordinarily the cantor comes to the rehearsal with sponsors to determine where best to stand to lead the singing, and to understand when the acclamations are sung. Timing is all important in this rite. The cantor needs to have the text of the rite along with any adaptations that will be made.

Music Director/Musician

The music director/musician is part of the rite's preparation and is given the text of the rite. The music director/musician takes a creative role in choosing appropriate songs and acclamations, and crafting the musical portions of the rite to meet the needs of the assembly. (See the sections on music, pp. 24 and 25.) If the music director/musician is not familiar with the rite, presence at the rehearsal is helpful to know exactly when the acclamations are sung.

Lectors

Lectors are very important at this rite because the Word proclaimed in the Sunday assembly is the Word that forms catechumens and candidates. Lectors need to know ahead of time if the Sunday readings or readings from the "Rite of Acceptance" are being used. Encourage them to proclaim the readings especially well. They need to know that the celebration of Mass will begin in a different way, and determine how the lectionary will get to the ambo. The intercessions are special ones for the catechumens and candidates. They may be read by a lector or someone else, or sung.

Hospitality Ministers

Hospitality ministers are especially important for the "Rite of Acceptance" or "Rite of Welcoming" because there will undoubtedly be family and friends from outside the parish community coming to support the catechumens and candidates. Hospitality ministers are available to greet all who come. They need to know any special seating arrangements, as they will assist people in finding appropriate seats and in gathering around the catechumens and their sponsors for the first part of the rite.

Engaging the Assembly

The entire parish community initiates new members. The initiation team is able to assist the community in knowing and living this truth. Because the rites usually take place within the Sunday assembly, the celebration of the rites is a significant time to encourage the community's participation. Various possibilities exist to help the community become more and more engaged in initiating new members.

Bulletin Announcement the Week Before Celebrating the *Rite of Acceptance* or the *Rite Welcoming*

Next Sunday at the *(time)* Mass we will welcome new members in our midst. *(Names of men, women, and children)* will be celebrating the "Rite of Acceptance into the Order of Catechumens." They are preparing for Baptism, Confirmation, and Eucharist. *(Names of already baptized men, women, and children)* already share our Christian faith through Baptism. They will celebrate the "Rite of Welcoming," as they mark this moment of following God's call to live their Christian faith and complete their initiation within the Catholic community.

The rite includes our going outside to welcome them as the Mass begins. They are signed by the cross of Christ and affirm their intention to live under Christ's cross. Their formation in God's Word begins as the Word we hear proclaimed each week in our assembly is presented to them. The Mass will take a little longer. You are important in this celebration and will welcome these men, women, and children into our midst and share your faith with them. After Mass you are invited to come to a reception in the parish hall to personally welcome and meet them.

Before coming next week, please give some thought to this question: "What is the cross you are embracing in your own life?" You may want to share your responses with your family or a friend before coming next Sunday.

Verbal Announcement at Mass the Week Before the Rite

Next week at the *(time)* Mass we will welcome into the catechumenate, those preparing for Baptism, those baptized in another Christian faith who seek full communion with us, and those Catholics who are baptized but never received any further formation and now seek Confirmation and Eucharist. Their names are in the bulletin. You are very important in this rite, for it is this whole parish community that is welcoming them, sharing our Christian faith with them, and walking the faith journey together in the days and years ahead. We hope as many as possible will be able to participate in this celebration. We will gather in the church as usual, but then will walk outside to meet them and bring them inside. Through their sponsors we all sign them with the cross of Christ; and we present a sacred treasure, God's Word that we hear proclaimed each week, to them to be their nourishment. We pray for them on their journey. After Mass you are invited to meet and greet them in a special reception.

As Christ's followers, we each embrace the cross. To prepare for this celebration, take some time this week to reflect on the cross you are embracing in your own life. You might want to share your reflections with a friend or with your family before coming next Sunday.

Prayer Sponsors

Invite parish members (individuals and/or families) to support a particular catechumen or candidate in prayer throughout the time of their initiation journey. Elicit these prayer sponsors through a bulletin or newsletter announcement. You might also encourage parish groups, for example, the parish council, Knights of Columbus, or St. Vincent de Paul Society, to support one or more catechumens and candidates in prayer. Each class in the parish school or religious formation program could be invited to pray for one of the catechumens or candidates. Give the name, picture, and some information about the individual for whom they are praying. Encourage the prayer sponsors to come to the reception after Mass and meet the person. They might also send a card or note of prayerful support at the time of the rite.

Newsletter

Provide a picture and some information about each of the inquirers who will be celebrating the "Rite of Acceptance" or "Rite of Welcoming." You may also ask each of these inquirers to write a statement about themselves and what drew them to the Catholic faith.

Vestibule or Bulletin Board

Place pictures with names of those who celebrate the "Rite of Acceptance" or "Rite of Welcoming" where they will be seen by the parish community.

Prayer

Include the inquirers who are celebrating the "Rite of Acceptance" or "Rite of Welcoming" in the parish's prayer in the following ways:

❖ Intercessions at Sunday Mass in the weeks before the rite.

❖ Intercessions at daily Mass during the week before the rite.

❖ Place the intention of their faith journey on the parish prayer chain.

❖ Have parish groups include these inquirers in their meeting's prayer.

C. Preparing the Rite

Environment

Most commonly, the "Rite of Acceptance" will be celebrated during Ordinary Time, but in any season the environment should reflect both the liturgical year and the natural world outside.

Inside the worship space, plants and hangings that accentuate the cross and ambo are appropriate. Attention should also be given to the gathering space, outside or near the doors of the church, where the first part of the rite takes place. Clear this space. Remove all clutter near the main entryway. If necessary, define the outdoor space with a few plants or festive banners in the color of the liturgical season.

Use an appropriate sound system. Most parishes have a portable sound system for outdoor use on Palm Sunday and other such occasions. If not, a system can be rented. Two microphones at minimum are desirable: a body mike for the presider and a hand-held microphone to pick up the voices of the sponsors and candidates during the opening dialogue.

Music

Here are some places where music can be used in this rite:

❖ A hymn or song when the assembly gathers.

❖ A sung antiphon as the assembly processes outdoors to surround the candidates and their sponsors.

❖ A sung response as each candidate is presented to the assembly.

❖ An acclamation at the first Acceptance of the Gospel.

❖ A response to the prayer "We praise you, Lord, and we bless you."

❖ An acclamation of joy as they are signed with the cross (to be repeated as each of the senses is signed with the cross).

❖ A sung antiphon as they go in to hear the Word of God. (This can be the same as the one sung as they processed out.)

- Music for the Liturgy of the Word follows the usual format for Sunday Mass, with a sung responsorial psalm and gospel acclamation.

- An acclamation as the Word is presented to each catechumen or candidate.

- Sung intercessions.

- Music as the catechumens go forth when they are dismissed.

Music Suggestions

Several resources offer specific ritual music for this rite. Most major hymnals and resources, such as those of Oregon Catholic Press, World Library Publications and GIA Publications, include responses and acclamations for this rite. The best known separate collection is David Haas's "Who Calls You by Name" (GIA Publications), which has become a byword for this ritual. Lynn Trapp (MorningStar) has composed a full setting of responses in a more classical vein, with parts for a singing presider and melodies for the assembly that can be dressed up with an SATB choir if one is available. Scott Soper's gospel style "Glory in the Cross" (from the collection "On That Day" [GIA Publications]) was composed for this rite and boasts a strong, rhythmic melody line that carries well both with and without accompaniment.

Another approach is to chose a familiar opening hymn to gather the assembly, and then take musical phrases from that hymn to serve as acclamations at various points in the ritual. The music of Taizé also offers highly singable antiphons that can be used for processions and acclamations.

Tips for Presiders

- Get to know the names of the sponsors and candidates who will be in the ritual. Although you will no doubt put them in your ritual text, it helps to be as free of that text as possible. Name tags are a crutch and should be avoided.

- Remember that many different people have a role in making this rite effective. Like a gracious maestro, you provide the cue for others to play their parts. Be aware of whose turn it is to speak, sing, move, and so on, and give your focused attention to the action as it takes place. If you are distracted or preoccupied (for example, paging through your notes while others are speaking), the assembly will become restless.

- If you plan to use your freedom to adapt the texts of the rite, prepare carefully what you are going to say, using those texts as a model. Internalize the meaning of what the text is trying to convey. Keep it simple.

- Remember that while the ritual is frequently focused on the candidates and their sponsors, the assembly should always be kept in mind. Make sure that you can be heard by all, that your gestures are big enough to be seen by all, and that your words and actions gather their prayers up.

- Set a lively pace, but do not be afraid of silence. Moments of quiet, a well-timed pause after something wonderful has been said, a deliberate gesture made without words will give people time to internalize what is going on. Liturgy is not a race against the clock; it is a way of stepping into God's time.

Homily Suggestions

Although this rite will most likely be celebrated on a Sunday, therefore automatically setting the Scripture texts upon which the homily will be based, it is worth taking the time to reflect upon and pray over the particular texts given for ritual Masses in the Lectionary (743). These texts, along with the dynamic of the rite itself, suggest how a homilist might approach preaching at this celebration. Read these Scriptures and pray over them. Take out the ritual text and contemplate not only its words but also the *praenotanda* (RCIA 36–38, 41–42, 47). Given what is being proclaimed in these Scriptures and celebrated in this rite, two major threads leap out: the idea of movement or threshold, and the idea of feasting at the table of God's Word.

Abram is commanded by God to go forth to a new land (Genesis 12:1–4). Jesus invites the disciples of John the Baptist to "come and see" where the Lord is staying—and presumably what he has to offer if they were to become his disciples (John 1:35–42). If nothing else, these Scriptures speak of a movement from something to something else. The promise of God opens up, is laid before the one who trusts in the Lord and who is willing to risk that movement in faith.

These candidates are certainly moving, at the most basic level, from the stage of the precatechumenate to the catechumenate.

Moving into the catechumenate presupposes a deeper internal movement arising from initial faith and conversion as candidates are drawn into the mystery of God's love (RCIA 37). They are answering the call to discipleship. The rite signifies this movement as they are signed with the cross and brought into the worshiping assembly.

Many Sunday Scriptures will lend themselves to this core theme of movement in faith, of a threshold being crossed over in life by the gentle grace and guidance of God. This is, after all, something that all of us continue to strive for as we mature in our discipleship.

No matter which set of Sunday Scriptures the homilist must preach, any can lend itself to the notion of feasting at the table of God's Word. In this ritual catechumens and candidates are invited to partake of the many riches laid before them, and before us, in the living Word of God.

Finally, while it is tempting to use the participants themselves, the catechumens and candidates, as a focus for the entire homily, it may be better to begin with the Scriptures, segue from them to the dynamic of the rite (movement or threshold or feasting upon the living Word), and conclude by referring to the catechumens and how they exemplify for all of us the conversion into which we are continually being invited.

Decisions That Need To Be Made

When Do We Celebrate This Rite?

Here are some considerations:

- ✧ The "Rite of Acceptance" may be celebrated several times during the year (RCIA 18.3). If the diocesan bishop has not fixed these days, they are determined according to the needs of the local community and the readiness of the inquirers.

- ✧ Of paramount importance is that the inquirers' precatechumenate has taken a sufficient time, and they are truly ready for this step (RCIA 18.8, 43). The criteria for their readiness are found in RCIA 42 (see also pp. 18 and 19 of this book and pp. 8 and 9 of the *Precatechumenate Manual* in this series, *Foundations in Faith*).

- ✧ The community must also be ready to celebrate. Sponsors have come forward for each and every candidate. The hospitality ministry is ready to create a welcoming atmosphere and host a reception. The assembly, through education, announcements and preaching, understands and can support what is taking place.

- ✧ Because of the central importance of the community's welcome in this rite, it seems ideal to celebrate it in the Sunday assembly, when the community gathers to celebrate the Eucharist. If another time is chosen, it should be an occasion when the community is fully represented (RCIA 45).

- ✧ A suitable time in the liturgical calendar and in the calendar of parish activities must be found. Many Sundays in Ordinary Time are excellent choices because of their emphasis on themes of discipleship. The celebratory seasons of Christmas and Easter can also be good times to celebrate this rite.

- ✧ Certain times should be avoided altogether. Lent is an inappropriate time because the rites of purification and enlightenment are the central focus. The first Sunday of Advent is an inappropriate time because the readings are about the end of the world. Days slated for pledge drives, outside speakers, and other sacramental celebrations are also days to avoid.

How Will the Assembly Be Active and Involved?

Here are some ideas:

- ✧ Gather the assembly with song and prayer and some words of explanation before greeting the inquirers and their sponsors, who are waiting at the doors.

- ✧ Invite the whole assembly to go outside, or at least to the threshold or entryway of the church, to surround the inquirers and show their support of them.

- ✧ Have the sponsors introduce the inquirers, rather than calling their names; have each sponsor keep a hand on his or her inquirer's shoulder throughout the rite to show the community's support.

- ✧ Have the inquirers respond to the questions in their own words (see the sections on the spiritual preparation of inquirers on p. 20) so that the assembly gets a sense of these people and their journey. Make certain that a working microphone is available to all who speak at any point in the rite.

✧ Use sung acclamations at key moments, such as the first Acceptance of the Gospel, the signing of the cross, and the giving of the Word.

✧ Make big gestures that all can see, especially when signing with the cross.

How Will We Highlight the Central Symbols?

Here are some ideas:

✧ Remember that the people themselves are central symbols in the rites of initiation. Be sure that they can be seen and heard and that their actions are simple and purposeful. A careful consideration of the space

available—outdoors, at the threshold of the church, and within the body of the church—will help to determine the movement and placement of people.

✧ The cross can be carried in procession when the assembly goes to meet the inquirers. This cross might even be presented for each inquirer to grasp in their hands as they make their first acceptance of the Gospel, thus highlighting their commitment.

✧ Make the most of the movement across the threshold into the church, with a clear invitation and joyful singing.

✧ Include *all* the signing of the senses as given in the ritual text; do not omit or reduce them.

✧ Any materials that are presented, such as Bibles or crosses, should be of good quality, carried and presented with dignity and reverence.

✧ The Liturgy of the Word should be a model of good proclamation and preaching that speaks to the occasion and opens up the meaning of the rite.

D. After the Rite

Evaluation of the Rite of Acceptance

Take time within ten days of celebrating the "Rite of Acceptance" or "Rite of Welcoming" to evaluate what went well, what did not, and what needs to be changed for the next celebration of this rite. Some people whom you may wish to involve in the evaluation are: the coordinator, the presider, the liturgist, the music director, and some additional team members. In addition to a core group of those who will reflect on the experience of this liturgy, input may be elicited from others in the parish.

A process similar to this one may be helpful:

1. Evaluators reflect on their experience, using the format on page 28, which may be duplicated as needed.
2. Each evaluator elicits responses from three parishioners who participated in this liturgy.
3. The evaluators come together to talk about their experiences and make appropriate suggestions for the next celebration of this (and possibly other) major rites.
4. The coordinator meets with appropriate persons to talk about these changes.

Evaluation: Rite of Acceptance, Rite of Welcoming

The rite celebrated was: _____ "Rite of Acceptance" _____ "Rite of Welcoming"

_____ "Combined Rite of Acceptance and Welcoming"

Date of celebration _____ Time of celebration _____

Number of catechumens _____ Number of candidates _____

1. For me the highlight of the rite was _____

   because _____ .

2. For me the part of the rite that was least meaningful was _____

   because _____ .

3. If I were to describe the important parts of this rite to others, I would tell them _____

   _____ .

4. Rate the following on a scale of 1–10 (1 is low, 10 is high) on how well
   this part of the rite was celebrated, and give a reason for your response.

   _____ Gathering and opening dialogue _____

   _____ The first acceptance of the Gospel _____

   _____ The signing of the senses _____

   _____ The presentation of the Word _____

   _____ The dismissal rite _____

   _____ The music that supported the liturgical action of the rite _____

   _____ The music was sung well by the assembly _____

5. If I were to change something in how this rite is celebrated the next time, I would suggest _____

   _____

   because _____ .

6. Other details that need to be remembered for the next celebration of the "Rite of Acceptance" or "Rite of Welcoming" are:

   _____

   _____

Mystagogy

Just as mystagogy is a whole period of time for neophytes to reflect on their experience of the Easter sacraments, each celebration of a liturgical rite merits mystagogical reflection. Mystagogical reflection gives those who have celebrated a rite a way to further take in and deepen their experience. Fuller appreciation of the rite comes as words are given to an experience. Likewise, a time of mystagogy fosters a theological understanding of the rite. (Consult the *Mystagogia Resource Book* in the *Foundations in Faith* series for a fuller understanding of mystagogy.) In the "Rite of Acceptance" or "Rite of Welcoming" a deeper sense of community, cross, discipleship, and the Word is often unfolded. Minimally, those men, women, and children who celebrated the rite should be given an opportunity for mystagogical reflection when they are dismissed during the rite. Those who were ministers at the rite, including the sponsors, the families of children, the lectors, the musicians, the cantors, the presider, the coordinator, the hospitality ministers, and part of the assembly may be invited at a later time to participate in some mystagogical reflection as well.

Mystagogical Reflection on the Rite of Acceptance or the Rite of Welcoming after the Dismissal

Gathering

1. Prepare the environment ahead of time using a cross, a space for the lectionary, and a candle.

2. Gather the participants. There will be a lot of excitement and energy. Ask the participants to say a word describing how they are feeling.

3. Invite everyone into a moment of quiet, and say this prayer: *Loving God, you have continued to call and form us as your people. We are grateful. Help us now take in all you want us to be aware of from the rite we just celebrated. Guide our time together. We pray in the name of Jesus, the one whom we follow. Amen.*

Remembering

1. Ask participants to share with the person next to them some of what touched them at the rite. (5 minutes)

2. Invite some sharing with everyone. Name the various parts of the liturgy, and invite a reflection on each part, one at a time. Include the following: standing and waiting, the community coming out to them, being introduced and invited to name what they want, acceptance of the Gospel and signing of the senses with the cross, processing into the worship space, hearing the Word and the homily, being presented with the Word, the intercessions, and the dismissal. Use active listening and reflective statements to encourage their deeper sharing.

3. Ask participants to reflect on this question: *What did this experience tell you about who God is, what the Church is, and what it means to be a disciple?* After a few minutes, invite responses.

Prayer

Close with a prayer of thanksgiving. Invite the participants to name something for which they are grateful. After each response, all say, We thank you, God.

Announcements

1. Remind the catechumens/candidates that this day marks the beginning of their entry into the catechumenate period, where they will be fed from the table of God's Word. Give specific information about when they will gather at Mass the following Sunday, sitting with their sponsors, dismissal and reflection, and the extended catechetical session.

2. As is appropriate, present them with one or more of the following to assist them in their catechumenal journey: A Catholic Bible (for anyone who does not have one), the *Remembrance Book*, the *Handbook on Prayer* (from the *Foundations in Faith* series), or a journal.

3. Invite them to go to the reception now.

Mystagogical Reflection for Liturgical Ministers, Assembly, and Catechumens/Candidates

Preparation

1. Invite the various ministers and the assembly at least a week before the rite takes place and again at announcement time the week of the rite. Tell parish groups at monthly meetings. Put the invitation in the bulletin and newsletter. Invite a cantor and/or musician to assist with the music.

2. Gather within a week of the rite in the church or another appropriate space. Provide a space for the processional cross and the lectionary.

3. Ask the cantor to lead everyone in singing the processional hymn/refrain used at the Mass.

Remembering

1. Invite participants to a moment of quiet and to recall the experience of the "Rite of Acceptance/Welcoming." Begin in this way: *As you gathered last Sunday, recall where you were sitting or standing, and who some of the people around you were. What were you aware of as the Mass began?* (Pause for a moment.) *Let your experience of this rite arise.* (As you name various moments of the rite, pause briefly between each to let their memories surface. Have the musician play or the cantor sing a line of the music used at appropriate places.) Continue: *We were invited to go and greet some men, women, and children. We walked to them and heard them introduced and their desire for God and Church. They accepted the Gospel and were signed with the cross. We processed with them into the church. We heard the Word of God.* (Here, insert a line or two from each of the readings and an image from the homily.) Continue: *God's Word was presented, we prayed for the new catechumens and candidates, and they were sent forth to further reflect on God's Word.* Pause for a moment, then invite everyone to open their eyes and become present to one another in this space.

2. Ask those present to respond to the following: *What is one part of the rite that spoke to you? Tell what you experienced. I ask you to keep your responses focused on this question. I'll remind you of this question periodically. Please stand and speak loudly enough so all can hear.* Take responses from many people. Keep them from getting into a discussion, critiquing, or talking about other experiences of Mass or the liturgy. One way to do this is to periodically repeat the invitation: *Name one part of the rite that spoke to you and tell what you experienced.*

3. Tell participants you are going to invite them to reflect on their experience in the light of their faith. Ask the following three questions, allowing a number of responses to each question before moving on to the next question.

   A. What did this liturgy speak to you about what God is like? What part of the rite told you that?

   B. What did this liturgy speak to you about what Church is? What part of the rite told you that?

   C. What did this liturgy speak to you about what it means to be a disciple? What part of the rite told you that?

4. Distribute a sheet of paper and a pencil to each person with the following two questions for reflection on it: *From this rite and this reflection, what do you want to remember for your faith journey? What do you sense God is wanting to tell you in your life?* Give participants a few minutes to write. Then, invite them to share something of their responses with the person next to them.

5. Invite some participants to speak aloud something they want to remember or something they sense God is telling them.

Prayer

1. Close with prayer. Begin: *As we conclude, let us pray for our catechumens and candidates.* (Name them.) Then pray the intercessions used at the "Rite of Acceptance" (RCIA 65). Adjust language to include candidates. Sing these if a cantor is available. Then say: *We were all claimed for Christ by the sign of his cross; let us now sign one another with the cross by turning to the person next to you and signing that person on the forehead.* Sing "All Are Welcome" (Haugen, GIA Publications).

Announcements

1. Invite participants to choose a particular catechumen or candidate to pray for during their catechumenate period.

2. Have copies of the *Remembrance Book* and the *Handbook on Prayer* available if anyone wishes to purchase them.

Note: The following reflection tool can be used in the bulletin or in various parish gatherings, e.g. parish council, education commission, St. Vincent de Paul.

Reflection on the Rite of Acceptance/Welcoming

If you were at the "Rite of Acceptance" or "Rite of Welcoming," take a few moments to reflect on your experience, using these questions. Share responses with your family or a friend.

1. What part of the rite spoke to you?
2. What did the rite say to you about who God is, what the Church is, and the meaning of discipleship?
3. What do you sense God wants to tell you from this rite?
4. Take a moment to pray for God's grace, and to pray for the catechumens and candidates.

Second Step: Election or Enrollment of Names

THE RITE OF SENDING
A. Overview of the Rite of Sending

The Rite at a Glance

LITURGY OF THE WORD

    Homily

    Presentation of the Catechumens

    Affirmation by the Godparents [and the Assembly]

    Intercessions for the Catechumens

    Prayer over the Catechumens

    Dismissal of Catechumens

LITURGY OF THE EUCHARIST

Understanding the Rite

The "Rite of Sending" is a rite devised to complement the "Rite of Election," strengthening those elements that may be weak or absent in the diocesan celebration and reinforcing elements common to both. To truly understand the "Rite of Sending," therefore, it is necessary to understand the "Rite of Election" (see the "Understanding the Rite" section of "Rite of Election," page 43).

The stated purpose of this rite, which exists only in the American version of the *Rite of Christian Initiation of Adults,* is to offer the parish's approval and support (RCIA 107) for those who are judged ready to go to the diocesan bishop for the "Rite of Election" (and/or the "Call to Continuing Conversion," for baptized candidates—another adaptation available for use in the U.S.). The "Rite of Sending" gives the parish community an

opportunity to publicly acknowledge and be involved in the second major transition in the initiation process that the "Rite of Election" represents, even when the bulk of the community cannot be present for the "Rite of Election" because it is celebrated at the cathedral or elsewhere under the presidency of the bishop.

The design of the ritual closely follows that of the "Rite of Election," from which it is derived. The **calling of each catechumen's name** aloud is an essential part of the "Rite of Election," and if it cannot be accomplished at the diocesan "Rite of Election," it takes place beforehand (RCIA 130) as in the "Rite of Sending." Often the calling of names occurs at both celebrations. **Affirmation by the godparents [and the assembly]** follows. The godparents' testimony, which represents the discernment of the whole community, is the basis on which the Church acts in electing these catechumens. **The godparents' role** is therefore the one most central to the rite. In the "Rite of Election," their affirmation is usually quite formal and occurs in the shape of questions with a unison response. This pattern is reproduced in the "Rite of Sending" (RCIA 112), but when the number of catechumens is small enough to make this practical, a popular adaptation is to have the godparents speak in their own words about the grace of God active in the life of each catechumen presented for election. Even members of the assembly may join in testifying to the readiness of these catechumens (RCIA 112). The presider concludes this part with a brief text that indicates that the parish sends these catechumens to the bishop to be elected.

Next the catechumens may **sign the Book of the Elect,** unless they are to do so later in the "Rite of Election" itself. Signing happens either at one rite or the other, but not both.

The act of signing the book is a gesture of commitment (RCIA 119) that the catechumens perform in response to God, who has in many times and places called them to become part of the chosen people. The gesture of signing concretizes the whole grace-laden event of God's call, to which the godparents have testified. The godparents too may sign the book (RCIA 123), as witnesses held accountable for the catechumens. The very concreteness of the book fixes the transcendent reality of God's eternal purposes firmly at one moment in time, experienced on the life journey of these individuals here and now. "Give in your names!" was the cry of the fourth century bishops who canvassed their congregations at the outset of Lent to find those ready to undergo Baptism at Easter. Today, by signing the Book of the Elect, modern day catechumens continue to "give in their names" for Baptism. By signing their names, they put themselves "on the line," sharing in the spirit of those early *competentes,* who petitioned eagerly for the sacraments of new life promised to them in Christ (RCIA 124).

Although the Book of the Elect may be signed in the parish "Rite of Sending," the **enrollment of names** takes place when the names are presented to the bishop in the "Rite of Election" itself. Once their names are enrolled, the bishop pronounces the **act of election** and entrusts them to the care of their **godparents,** who at that moment officially take up their lifelong role. These three elements, reserved strictly to the "Rite of Election," show the distinction between the two rites. So zealous is the ritual text to protect the unique role of the bishop in the "Rite of Election" that the catechumens are not called the elect in the "Rite of Sending" but only once the act of election is spoken by the bishop or his delegate in the "Rite of Election."

In the "Rite of Sending," as in the "Rite of Election," **intercessions** are prayed, and they may take the place of the general intercessions. The intercessions name the various groups who have participated in the initiation journey. The intercessions conclude with a **prayer over the catechumens,** with hands extended. The catechumens are then dismissed from the assembly.

Baptized Candidates: What's Different?

Baptized candidates who will be sent for recognition by the bishop in the "Call to Continuing Conversion," which is their rite parallel to the "Rite of Election," also participate in the "Rite of Sending," either according to the "Rite of Sending" for candidates only (RCIA 434 ff.) or, if there are both candidates and catechumens, according to the combined rite (RCIA 530 ff.). Sponsors, rather than godparents, offer the affirmation, and it includes specific mention of the candidates' Baptism. The candidates do not sign the Book of the Elect. These rites do not dismiss the baptized candidates. Otherwise the ritual pattern and even the prayer texts are virtually identical with the rite for catechumens.

According to the chapter on uncatechized adults (RCIA 400 ff.), baptized candidates who do not have godparents select them during the catechumenate period (RCIA 404), and these godparents fulfill the same responsibilities as do the godparents of the catechumens. All of the adapted rituals for baptized candidates completely ignore this directive, however, and speak only of sponsors for the candidates, never of godparents. This inconsistency in the ritual text has resulted in the practice of not assigning godparents to candidates.

What About Children?

Although the American edition of the ritual book offers an optional "Rite of Election" for children, no mention is made of children's participation in the "Rite of Sending." Nevertheless, it seems advisable to include children in every stage of the process, and if they are included in the "Rite of Election," it would make no sense to exclude them from the parish "Rite of Sending." As the texts of the children's adaptation of the "Rite of Election" show, very little adaptation specific to children is envisioned anyway, and in mixed groups the adult rite is followed (RCIA 279). On the practical level, planners should be aware that children, especially young children, need significantly more time than adults to sign the Book of the Elect.

B. Preparing the Community

Discernment before the Rite of Sending

The *Rite of Christian Initiation of Adults* places a strong emphasis on discernment before the "Rite of Election" or the "Call to Continuing Conversion" for which the "Rite of Sending" prepares. At this time the Church determines the readiness of catechumens and candidates to be called to the Easter sacraments, who will normally have had about a year of formation in the catechumenate period (RCIA, NS 6). The broader church community is involved in this discernment process, including catechumens, candidates, team members, sponsors, the bishop, priests, deacons, catechists, and other members of the community (RCIA 121 and 122). Godparents and sponsors are asked to give testimony during the "Rite of Sending" and to affirm the catechumens' or candidates' readiness again in the "Rite of Election" and "Call to Continuing Conversion" with the diocesan bishop. Their participation in discernment helps to prepare the godparents and sponsors for their testimony (RCIA 123). The *Rite of Christian Initiation of Adults* notes particular signs of readiness for celebrating this rite (RCIA 120). The catechumens and candidates are to:

❖ be converted in mind and in action,

❖ be adequately familiar with Christian beliefs, and

❖ live in a spirit of faith and charity.

The Discernment Process

About six weeks before the celebration of the "Rite of Sending" the coordinator sets in motion a time of discernment regarding readiness in catechumens and candidates for the Easter sacraments. Individual interviews may be scheduled with specific areas of discernment discussed. Involving godparents and sponsors, catechists, and other team members in a discernment process is both necessary and desirable.

Discernment Day or Evening

One way to involve a group in discernment is to hold a day or evening gathering for this purpose. An individual interview with each catechumen and candidate has already occurred. The coordinator gathers those who are participating in the discernment. This includes team members, sponsors, godparents,

---

Sample Reflection Questions for Catechumens and Candidates

❖ In what ways do you see life differently than when you began this journey?

❖ What changes have you made in your life at home or at work?

❖ How would you describe the role God plays in your life?

❖ In what ways are you more a part of the parish community?

❖ What have you discovered in service to those in need?

❖ How has your desire for the sacraments moved in you?

❖ What do you ask God to help you change?

Sample Reflection for Catechists and Team Members

Provide a list of catechumens and candidates. Spend some time reflecting on each of these catechumens and candidates. Recall catechetical sessions and other ways you have interacted with them. After each name, write some thoughts about how you have seen the person:

❖ respond to God's Word.

❖ deepen a sense of Christian values in daily life.

❖ develop as a person of prayer.

❖ reach out to others in service.

❖ be a willing participant in the Christian community.

Write down any concerns or hesitations about initiating these catechumens and candidates this Easter.

What is your particular hope or prayer for each of these catechumens and candidates?

Sample Reflection Questions for Sponsors

❖ Recall some of the recent Sunday gospel texts we have reflected on together. What impact have you noticed these have had in the person you are sponsoring? Give one or two examples.

❖ What are some of the ways you have seen the person you are sponsoring change?

❖ In what ways does this person live the Christian faith through prayer, in service, and in sharing their faith with others?

❖ In what further area(s) do you sense God may be inviting the person you are companioning to change?

❖ How have you heard the person you are sponsoring talk about their desire for the Easter sacraments?

❖ Do you have any concerns or hesitation about initiating the person this Easter?

❖ What is your hope and prayer for the person you are sponsoring?

and perhaps other members of the community who know the catechumens or candidates. Some parishes choose to involve the catechumens and candidates in this gathering. The context for this discernment is prayer, a time of listening to the truth of how God is moving in the person. This truth before God may indicate readiness for movement to the initiation sacraments, or that more time for formation is needed. Begin with prayer. With a sense of reverence and confidentiality, bring forth the name of each catechumen and candidate individually. Have the sponsor/godparent and any others who have observed signs of

readiness in this person or who have concerns share these aloud. If catechumens and candidates are present, they share their impressions of how God has moved in them and any areas of growth still needed. All hold this person in prayer. After listening in silence, the coordinator (or another with these skills) summarizes the truth heard. A determination is made of whether the signs of readiness are present or whether additional time is needed. Then the next person's name is brought forward. When the discernment seems clear, the time ends in prayer. After this gathering, further communication is needed with each catechumen and candidate.

Spiritual Preparation of Catechumens/Candidates for the Rite of Sending

Note: You may wish to gather for this session on an evening or Saturday morning before the "Rite of Sending" occurs. This session takes both catechumens and candidates into account. You may separate them, with the candidates gathering near the baptismal font.

Gathering

1. Prepare the environment, using purple and white cloths, a lighted candle, and an open Bible. Invite catechumens and candidates to sit by their sponsors.

2. Sing together "I Have Loved You" (Joncas, NALR). Provide copies.

3. Continue the prayer with these or similar words: *Loving and gracious God, we are here because you have chosen us. You have drawn us into your life. You have taught us your ways. You have given us the riches only you can offer. We are grateful. Enlighten our minds and hearts with a fuller knowledge of who you are, and who we are with you. We pray through Christ, the One who shows us the way to you. Amen.*

Reflection

1. Give this introduction to the reading: *Those who await Baptism have been called to live in Christ's light. During our journey these months, God has transformed us. Those who are baptized—sponsors, candidates, team members—are also being transformed as our Baptism lives more fully in us. We are all people who live surrounded by the light of Christ. Listen for the words in this reading from*

Ephesians that speak personally to you. Have a team member proclaim Ephesians 5:8–20.

2. Elicit words and phrases from everyone.

3. Give handouts to everyone with the following questions on them. Then play some reflective background music (20 minutes).

   A. As you are aware of God's love for you, what are three ways this love has moved you to change?

   B. What gifts of God might others recognize in you?

   C. What does it mean for you to live in Christ's light?

4. Invite catechumens and candidates and their sponsors to share their reflection in pairs (15 minutes).

5. Gather everyone together and invite each pair to share one part of their reflection.

6. Proclaim Ephesians 5:8–20 again.

Prayer

1. Make the following statement: *We are all here because of God, because of God's goodness and love, because God chooses us to live in this goodness and love. Think of something for which you want to thank and bless God.* (Pause). Then state: *We will pray together, completing the phrase "God, I thank you for . . ."* After each statement, we will sing: *"Blessed be God, O Blessed be God"* (from "Who Calls You By Name," Haas, GIA Publications).

2. Conclude by singing "We Are Called" (Haas, GIA Publications).

Announcements

1. Tell everyone where to gather for the "Rite of Sending."

2. Invite everyone to the reception after the "Rite of Sending."

3. If sponsors have not yet had their rehearsal, tell sponsors when the rehearsal will be.

4. Remind everyone about the details for the diocesan "Rite of Election" and "Call to Continuing Conversion."

Preparing the Ministers

Sponsors and Godparents

The ministry of the sponsor continues to unfold. By this time the sponsor will have developed a trusting relationship with the catechumen or candidate. The sponsor will also have participated in the discernment for "Rite of Election" or the "Call to Continuing Conversion." At the "Rite of Sending," the ministry of godparent begins for those accompanying catechumens, and sponsors continue to accompany the baptized candidates. Godparents and sponsors participate in a rehearsal for the "Rite of Sending." Some things they need to know about their role in this rite are:

✧ They meet the catechumen or candidate and take the person to the appropriate place in the worship space.

✧ The godparent or sponsor physically supports and maintains contact with the person throughout the rite by keeping a hand on the person's shoulder or arm through the rite.

✧ The rite occurs after the homily.

✧ The godparent or sponsor is asked to give testimony, either in the form of a response or statements about the person (according to the parish's determination).

✧ The godparent accompanies the catechumen when called to sign the Book of the Elect.

✧ The sponsor accompanies the candidate when called to come forward.

✧ Godparents and sponsors may be asked to place their hands on the shoulders of the person through the time of the intercessions.

✧ At the time of dismissal, godparents and sponsors stay in the church for the remainder of Mass.

✧ After Mass, godparents and sponsors meet with the catechumens and candidates and take them to the parish reception.

✧ The godparents and sponsors go with the catechumen or candidates to the (arch)diocesan celebration of the "Rite of Election" and "Call to Continuing Conversion."

✧ Directions communicated about this rite from the (arch)diocesan office are given to the godparents and sponsors. Normally they will sit with the catechumens and candidates, stand with them, and in some cases accompany them to the sanctuary.

Presider

The presider will know the catechumens and candidates and will have participated in some way in the discernment. Before the rehearsal for the "Rite of Sending" the presider is given the text for the rite, with appropriate names for the catechumens and their godparents, and the candidates and their sponsors. Options in the rite and placement in the worship space are determined before the rehearsal. The liturgist, the coordinator, or the presider leads the rehearsal with the godparents and sponsors. After walking through the rite, further clarifications are made in the text.

Coordinator

The coordinator is at the rehearsal and shares any pertinent information. On the day of the rite, the coordinator comes early to the church and makes sure everything is in place, including the Book of the Elect, if it is to be signed in the parish, with two working pens. The coordinator greets and reassures the catechumens and godparents, and the candidates and sponsors. The coordinator may be involved in the rite in one or more of the following ways: presenting the catechumens and candidates, moving between godparents and sponsors with a microphone for the testimony, assisting in movement to sign the Book of the Elect, cuing in the presider for any missed names or people, and processing with the Book of the Elect through the assembly.

The coordinator or a catechist will lead the catechumens out after the intercessions and reflect with them on their experience of the rite (see "Mystagogy," pp. 41 and 42). When the celebration of Mass is over, the coordinator sees to it that the catechumens and candidates are taken to the reception.

Cantor

The cantor is once again important in bringing the entire assembly into the celebration of the rite with the sung acclamations. Participating in the rehearsal with the godparents and sponsors is helpful to understand the timing for singing the acclamations. The cantor needs to have the text of the rite.

Music Director/Musician

The music director/musician is part of the rite's preparation and is provided with the text of the rite. The music director takes a creative role in choosing appropriate songs and acclamations and in crafting the musical portions of the rite to meet the needs of the assembly. If the music director/musician is not familiar with this rite, his or her presence at the rehearsal is helpful to understand where the acclamations occur.

Lectors

This rite normally occurs on the First Sunday of Lent. The lectors need to know that the Liturgy of the Word occurs in the normal fashion with the "Rite of Sending" occurring after the homily. The intercessions (whether read by a lector or someone else, or sung) are special ones for the catechumens and candidates.

Hospitality

Hospitality ministers are informed about the "Rite of Sending" ahead of time. They will need to be alert to places reserved for those participating in the rite, and for the family and friends visiting for this celebration. Hospitality ministers are available to greet all who come.

Engaging the Assembly

The entire community is called to support the catechumens and candidates. It does so in various ways. The Mass in which the catechumens and candidates participate has a regular assembly, which will be well aware of the initiation journey. The assembly at all Masses will have been praying for the catechumens and candidates at the time of the intercessions. Some members of the parish community may participate in the discernment of readiness for those catechumens and candidates celebrating this rite. All of the community needs to know about this rite and be invited to participate in the rite and the reception. Some communities find it helpful to celebrate this rite at more than one Mass so that a greater number of parishioners can participate.

Bulletin Announcement the Week Before Celebrating the Rite of Sending for Election or for the Call to Continuing Conversion

Next Sunday at the *(time)* Mass we will celebrate the "Rite of Sending for Election" with our catechumens *(names of men, women, and children)*. We will celebrate the "Rite of Sending for the Call to Continuing Conversion" with our baptized candidates *(names)*. The Church has discerned their readiness for reception of the initiation sacraments this Easter. After these rites are celebrated here next Sunday morning, these catechumens and candidates, along with their godparents and sponsors, will be sent by our parish to the (arch)bishop for the "Rite of Election" (for the catechumens) and "Call to Continuing Conversion" (for the candidates). Based on the testimony given by the sponsors and our support of their readiness for the sacraments, the (arch)bishop will declare the catechumens to be elect, chosen by God for the sacraments this Easter. The (arch)bishop also recognizes the desire of the baptized candidates for the sacraments of Confirmation and Eucharist within the Catholic community.

Before coming next week, recall how you have seen God alive in any of the catechumens and candidates you know. Reflect also on ways God has molded you as God's own. Ask yourself: What gifts of God have others told you they recognize in you? Share your responses with your family or a friend before next Sunday.

After Mass you are invited to participate in a reception in the parish hall to celebrate God's action in our catechumens and candidates.

On *(date and time)* you are encouraged to participate in a time of reflection on your experience of the "Rite of Sending" as we together discover more fully what God is doing in our midst.

Verbal Announcement at Mass the Week Before the Rite

Next week at the *(time)* Mass we will celebrate the "Rite of Sending for Election" with our catechumens and the "Rite of Sending for the Call to Continuing Conversion" with our baptized candidates. We have been praying for them during the intercessions, at various parish gatherings, and when they are dismissed weekly after the homily. In recent weeks we have discerned their readiness for the initiation sacraments this Easter. We celebrate what God has done and is doing in them. It is the fruit of God's action that we see. It gives evidence that they are truly chosen by God for the sacraments of Baptism, Confirmation, and Eucharist. We encourage any who are able to, to come to this *(time)* Mass. Though Mass will be a little longer than usual, it is a wonderful opportunity for our community to celebrate the gifts God is giving in these men, women, and children in our midst.

Prayer Sponsors

Contact individual and group prayer sponsors, and classmates of children preparing for initiation. Alert them to the celebration of the "Rite of Sending." Invite them to come to the Mass and reception when this rite is celebrated. They may wish to send a card or note of support and prayer at this time.

Newsletter

After the discernment has taken place, write an article for the parish newsletter. Include the names of the catechumens who will celebrate the "Rite of Election" and their godparents, and the names of the candidates who will celebrate the "Rite of Sending for the Call to Continuing Conversion" and their sponsors. Ask each sponsor and godparent to write a statement about the ways in which God has acted in the catechumen or candidate during the catechumenate. Invite the parish to hold these men, women, and children in prayer during the time of this rite and particularly through the coming season of preparation.

Vestibule or Bulletin Board

Update the pictures displayed with special acknowledgment of those celebrating the "Rite of Sending" and their godparents and sponsors.

Prayer

Include these men, women, and children and their godparents and sponsors in prayer in intercessions at Sunday, daily, and school Masses, in prayer at parish meetings, and on the parish prayer chain.

Environment

The environment for the "Rite of Sending" normally accords with Lent, whose environment is simple to the point of austerity and the color purple predominates. (If the rite is celebrated before the outset of Lent, of course, the green of Ordinary Time would be used.)

If the parish has a Book of the Elect, the book should have a visible resting place, even if the book is to be signed later, in the "Rite of Election." One possibility is a central location in the midst of the assembly, where it can be signed and all can see it. Another is a location near the baptismal font, provided the font is within view. If candles are set near the stand on which the book is displayed, they could be lighted after the book is signed and remain standing as a continuing reminder to the parish that the rite has taken place and that the book now holds the names of the elect.

Music

Most of the traditional repertoire for the First Sunday of Lent—and indeed for the entire Lenten season—emphasizes penitence, with little or no suggestion of the themes of preparation for Baptism or renewal of Baptism that are so important to the renewed liturgy. A challenge to music planners is to find a strong opening hymn for the "Rite of Sending" that brings forward the initiation context of Lent.

Equally challenging is the task of identifying music that speaks in a robust way of the mystery of divine election. Election is outward-directed; a person is elected for mission. Yet oftentimes songs about being the chosen of God wax sentimental and take an individualistic tone. Election music should be jubilant and hope-filled. It acclaims God's wonderful purposes in the work of salvation through the creation of a people that are to be salt and light for the world. It revels in the paradox of God's call to the humble and the lowly. Music about election, while it gives full emphasis to God's gracious initiative, also appropriately voices the human response—our yes to God's election.

If individual testimony is offered for each catechumen, a sung acclamation after each affirmation can highlight what is taking place. Alternatively, an acclamation can punctuate the signing of

the book. If there are many to sign the book, a responsorial psalm or a song with a refrain would be a better choice (an acclamation repeated too many times can become tedious). The rubrics for the enrollment of names in the "Rite of Election" suggest Psalm 16 or Psalm 33 with the refrain "Happy the people the Lord has chosen to be his own" (RCIA 132). The subheading for the section of the ritual book entitled "Second Step: Election or Enrollment of Names" is taken from the liturgy for the First Sunday of Lent, Year B, and would also be a fine choice: "Your ways, O Lord, are love and truth, to those who keep your covenant" (Psalm 25). Music with a sung refrain both engages the people and allows them to attend to the liturgical action. The same is true for the moment when the book is shown to the assembly. If such an adaptation is used, it should certainly be accompanied by music, but not music that keeps the assembly's eyes on a printed text.

Music Suggestions

Some appropriate hymns and songs for the "Rite of Sending" might be:

- ✧ "From Ashes to the Living Font" (tune: St. Flavian, GIA Publications)
- ✧ "Lift High the Cross" (tune: Crucifer, GIA Publications)
- ✧ "Jerusalem My Destiny" (Cooney, GIA Publications)
- ✧ "We Are Called" (Haas, GIA Publications)
- ✧ "For the Life of the World" (Haas, GIA Publications)
- ✧ "Sign Me Up" (Yancy and Metcalfe, GIA Publications)
- ✧ "Digo Si, Señor" (Peña, GIA Publications)

(For psalmody to accompany the liturgical action, see the section "Music" on this page.)

Acclamations for this rite may be found in many hymnals. The title song of the David Haas collection "Who Calls You by Name" (GIA Publications) is noteworthy.

Homily Suggestions

A number of important points will be highlighted in this homily and because at least one of them is future oriented, the entire project of preaching will be a challenge. The homilist must first address the Sunday Scriptures and draw out of them a pertinent message about our fundamental call to be God's chosen people and our response of following of the Lord Jesus that would speak to any believer attending Mass. In addition, he will also speak to the experience of the catechumens and candidates and how their initiation process is entering the proximate stage for celebration of the initiation sacraments (keeping in mind that *how* that happens for catechumens and candidates is different, respecting their baptismal status). Finally, some mention of the rite that will follow—which is a preparation for the "Rite of Election" with the bishop, is needed, understanding that the referent, for the homilist, is a future event that does not take place within the parish.

The rite itself may assist in preparing such a multileveled homily. The notes that precede the combined rite shed light on the character of the parish "Rite of Sending." The bishop is the visible sign of unity within a particular Church. Therefore, it is fitting that the catechumens and candidates are sent to him. The "local Church" is not the parish. It is the diocese, with the bishop as its head. However, the parish community bears responsibility for preparing catechumens and candidates for the fullest possible life within the local Church.

The homilist, therefore, may want to focus on the concrete worship experience, the daily witness and the ministry or outreach of the parish through which the catechumens and candidates follow their election and deepen their appreciation of the Church's tradition and universal nature. Most Catholics (those who do not work in the curia in Rome) experience the universal church "up close and personal" in their parish—each of which is just a small part of a larger diocese.

To what are the catechumens and candidates being sent? To the bishop who will speak for the local Church, the diocese, which, in turn, speaks for God. Having celebrated with the bishop, they will return to the parish and continue to move closer to the celebration of the initiation sacraments by participating in the rich life of the Church, which is manifested in our neighborhoods, our ministry close to home, our worship, our witness. We respond to the voice of Christ, who is so very close to us, calling us to faithful lives—right here.

Decisions That Need To Be Made

When Do We Celebrate this Rite?

Here are some considerations:

✧ According to the ritual text, the "Rite of Sending" is celebrated prior to the "Rite of Election" "at a suitable time" (RCIA 108). The best time for this celebration may be the First Sunday of Lent, in order to anchor this parish event in Lent, the liturgical season in which the implications of the catechumens' election unfold. The Sundays of Lent, from the viewpoint of Christian initiation, properly begin with the mystery of election; and this rite is the parish's component in election.

✧ Nevertheless, because it may be difficult or even impossible to celebrate the "Rite of Sending" on the First Sunday of Lent because of travel, scheduling needs of the diocese, and so on, another Sunday prior to the "Rite of Election" could be suitable. It would be important to check the lectionary readings for suitability as well. Because of the community's role in the "Rite of Sending" (see RCIA 107), it makes sense to celebrate this rite at a prime time when the community gathers, such as the principal Sunday liturgy.

✧ If Sunday Mass proves problematic, the "Rite of Sending" may be held at a celebration of the Word of God (RCIA 109). This would allow the freedom to select readings appropriate to the theme of election. Care should be exercised to see that the whole parish, and not just a small group, gathers at such a rite so that the catechumens are truly sent to the bishop with a full sense of community support.

✧ If there are many catechumens, the rite could be celebrated at more than one liturgy. This would allow sufficient time for individual testimony and to share with as many parishioners as possible the discernment that has taken place.

How Will We Highlight the Central Symbols?

Here are some ideas:

✧ The catechumens themselves are a central symbol of the rite. Their names should be called clearly, deliberately and slowly; and the catechumens should be presented to the assembly in such a way that their faces are visible, so that everyone can see who is being called and learn what their names are. If they sign the Book of the Elect, the action should be clearly seen.

✧ The godparents and their testimony (affirmation) are also central to the rite. According to the *praenotanda* of the "Rite of Election," the godparents' names are called along with those of the catechumens (RCIA 123, 130). Although the rubrics for the "Rite of Sending" omit mention of this, it makes even better sense to acknowledge them by name in the "Rite of Sending."

✧ The godparents' testimony should be well-considered and delivered so that all can hear. If the godparents are prepared to put the affirmation in their own words, so much the better. But even if they use a formula, they should internalize its meaning. Prior to the rite, the godparents take part in the discernment of the catechumens' readiness. Their ritual action in giving testimony therefore can be most authentic.

✧ The action of signing the Book of the Elect—and indeed the way in which the book itself is presented, handled, displayed and carried—should be dignified and reverent. The book can be carried aloft in the entrance procession by a catechist and should be displayed open, on a beautiful stand (near to the font, if possible) when it is not in use. Processing around the church with the book and "showing" the names to the assembly after the book has been signed is another popular adaptation to enhance the symbol of the book.

How Will the Assembly be Active and Involved?

Here are some ideas:

✧ The assembly, as well as the godparents, takes part in the discernment of readiness by sharing their observations of the catechumens prior to the rite. The ritual allows for the assembly to express their affirmation publicly in the rite (RCIA 112), but it does not indicate how this is done. A fertile field for adaptation is open here. The opportunity to give individual verbal testimony can be opened to anyone from the assembly, or the assembly as a whole may be asked to speak or sing an affirmation together, or it may applaud or convey its affirmation through some other nonverbal gesture. This is such a wordy rite on the whole that a symbolic action involving the whole assembly would be welcome. Considerations of culture will also suggest what is an appropriate expression of affirmation.

✧ Appropriate music is always helpful in engaging the assembly (see section on music, p. 37).

✧ One weakness of the ritual text is that it offers no words of invitation to introduce the signing of the book. Some words need to be crafted here both to signal to the catechumens that they are invited to give their names and to help the assembly know what is happening.

D. After the Rite

Evaluation of the Rite of Sending

Take some time within ten days of celebrating the "Rite of Sending" to evaluate what went well, what did not, and what needs to be changed for the next celebration of this rite. Some people you may wish to involve in the evaluation are: the coordinator, the presider, the liturgist, the music director, and some additional team members. In addition to a core group of those who will reflect on the experience of this liturgy, input may be elicited from others in the parish.

A process similar to this may be helpful:

1. Evaluators reflect on their experience, using the format on page 40 which may be duplicated as needed.
2. Each evaluator elicits responses from three parishioners who participated in this liturgy.
3. The evaluators come together to talk about their experiences and make appropriate suggestions for the next celebration of this (and possibly other) major rites.
4. The coordinator meets with appropriate persons to talk about possible changes.

Evaluation: Rite of Sending

The rite celebrated was: _____ The "Rite of Sending for Election"

_____ The "Rite of Sending for the Call to Continuing Conversion"

_____ The Combined Rite

Date of celebration _____ Time of celebration _____

Number of catechumens _____   Number of candidates _____

1. For me the highlight of the rite was _____

    because _____ .

2. For me the part of the rite that was least meaningful was _____

    because _____ .

3. If I were to describe the important parts of this rite to others, I would tell them _____

    _____ .

4. Rate the following on a scale of 1–10 (1 is low, 10 is high) on how well
   this part of the rite was celebrated and give a reason for your response.

    _____ The affirmation by godparents/sponsors _____

    _____ The signing of the book by catechumens _____

    _____ The recognition of candidates _____

    _____ The dismissal rite _____

    _____ The music supported the liturgical action of the rite _____

    _____ The music was sung well by the assembly _____

5. If I were to change something in how this rite is celebrated the next time, I would suggest _____

    _____

    because _____

    _____ .

6. Other details that need to be remembered for the next celebration of the "Rite of Sending" are:

    _____

    _____

    _____

Mystagogy

The mystagogical reflection following the dismissal at the parish "Rite of Sending" is found in the *Foundations in Faith, Resource Book for Purification and Enlightenment.*

Mystagogical Reflection on the Rite of Sending, for Liturgical Ministers, Assembly, Elect/Candidates, and Godparents/Sponsors

Preparation

1. Invite the various ministers and the assembly at least a week before the rite takes place, and again at announcement time the week of the rite. Tell parish groups at monthly meetings. Put the invitation in the bulletin and newsletter. Invite a cantor and/or musician to assist with the music.

2. Gather in the church or another appropriate space during the week after the rite. Include in the environment a large lighted candle, the Book of the Elect, and the Lectionary. If the Book of the Elect is signed at the diocesan rite, you may wish to borrow it for this reflection.

Gathering

1. Welcome everyone. Ask them to greet those seated nearby.

2. Ask the cantor to lead everyone in singing "We Are Called" (Haas, GIA Publications).

Remembering

1. Invite participants into a moment of quiet and to recall the experience of the "Rite of Sending." Begin in this way: *Recall where you were seated and what was in your awareness as Sunday's Mass began. It was the First Sunday of Lent, and you may have noticed the colors or environment prepared for this season. We sang, prayed the Kyrie, and listened to God's Word.* (Here insert a line or two from each of the readings, and an image from the homily.) Continue: *We heard the godparents and sponsors speak for each of the elect and candidates.* (You may include some key words

from the testimony that was offered.) Continue: *The elect signed the Book of the Elect.* (Omit this if the book is not signed at the parish. You may include here a sung refrain of an acclamation that was used.) *The candidates were recognized. The Book of the Elect was reverently shown to the community. We prayed for the elect and candidates and sent them forth to reflect on God's rich Word.*

2. Ask those present to respond to the following: *What is one part of the rite that spoke to you? Tell what you experienced. I ask you to keep your responses focused on this question. I'll remind you of this question periodically. Please stand and speak loudly enough so all can hear.*

3. Take responses from many people. Keep them from discussing, critiquing, or talking about other experiences of Mass or the liturgy. Periodically repeat the invitation: *Name one part of the rite that spoke to you and tell what you experienced.*

4. Then state the following: *Now we are going to reflect on our experience in the light of our faith.* Ask these three questions, allowing a number of responses to each question before moving on to the next question:
   A. What did this liturgy say to us about what God is like?
   B. What did this liturgy say to us about the meaning of being chosen or elected by God?
   C. What did this liturgy say to us about what it means to be Church?

5. Give a sheet of paper to everyone with the following two questions for reflection on it:

   A. Recall that all the baptized are chosen/elected by God in our Baptism. Picture your name in the Book of the Elect. How does being chosen/elected by God affect your daily life?

   B. Imagine yourself being personally called by God to walk in the light of Christ. In what way(s) do you desire to follow Christ more fully?

6. When everyone is finished, invite participants to share something of their responses to the person next to them.

7. Invite some participants to speak aloud something they discovered through tonight's reflection.

Prayer

1. Invite the godparents to place a hand on the shoulder of the elect and to come together into the midst of the gathered community. Make the following statement: *As we conclude, let us pray for* (names of the elect) *who are chosen by God and elected for the sacraments of Baptism, Confirmation, and Eucharist at this coming Easter Vigil.* Pray the intercessions from the "Rite of Election" (RCIA 134A) in spoken or sung form. Have the godparents and the elect return to their places.

2. Invite the sponsors to place a hand on the shoulder of the candidates and to come together into the midst of the gathered community. Make the following statement: *Let us pray for* (names of candidates) *who are already chosen by God in their Baptism and who now embark on this last step of their journey to Confirmation, Eucharist, and full communion in the Catholic Church.* Pray the intercessions from the "Rite of Election" (RCIA 134B) in spoken or sung form, adapting the language as necessary. Have the sponsors and the candidates return to their places.

3. Have a lector or team member proclaim Ephesians 5:8–20.

4. Sing together "Out of Darkness" (Walker, OCP).

Announcements

1. Tell everyone about the upcoming scrutiny celebrations and any preparation sessions they are welcome to participate in. Encourage them to keep the elect and candidates in prayer.

2. Have copies of the *Remembrance Book* and the *Handbook on Prayer* available if anyone wishes to purchase them to further their Lenten prayer and reflection.

Note: This reflection tool can be used in the bulletin or in various parish gatherings.

Reflection on the *Rite of Sending*

If you were at the "Rite of Sending," take a few moments to reflect on your experience using these questions. Share responses with your family, a friend, or a fellow parish journeyer:

1. What moved you in the "Rite of Sending"?

2. What did the rite say to you about who God is, what the Church is, and what it means to be elected by God?

3. What is one way God is inviting you to live in Christ's light more fully?

4. Take a moment to ask God for this grace. Pray for the elect and the candidates.

The Rite at a Glance

LITURGY OF THE WORD

    Homily

    Presentation of the Catechumens

    Affirmation by the Godparents [and the Assembly]

    Invitation and Enrollment of Names

    Act of Admission or Election

    Intercessions for the Elect

    Prayer over the Elect

    Dismissal of the Elect

LITURGY OF THE EUCHARIST

Understanding the Rite

The "Rite of Election" is a celebration of God's call to each person who approaches the Easter sacraments. It is God who calls and chooses a people to be his own. The Church confirms and gives voice to this sacred reality through all the rites of initiation. The "Rite of Election" stands out among all these rites, however, as a signal opportunity for the Christian community to name and affirm the work of God in its midst, as God forms a people for service to the mission of Christ. This rite is so important that the bishop himself presides over it, even though he may be unable to celebrate the sacraments of initiation. Election is called the hinge or pivot of the whole initiation process.

In the Biblical tradition the chosen people of Israel was marked out to bear special witness to God's power, goodness, and love, not because of their innate superiority, but simply through the unmerited favor of God. The Christian community carries on this witness to God's gracious initiative in the spirit of the good news that while we were still sinners, Christ died for us. The "Rite of Election" is therefore never an occasion for self-congratulation, but is always an affirmation of the grace of God.

The rite is comprised of several elements: the Liturgy of the Word, the presentation of candidates, the testimony of godparents, the

election, the entrusting of the elect to the care of their godparents, the intercessions, and the prayer over the elect. While the parish "Rite of Sending" duplicates some of these elements, the "Rite of Election" is the unique occasion for the enrollment, the act of election, and the commencement of the new role of the godparents.

The godparents and their affirmation are of crucial importance to this rite. Without their testimony, the Church, in the person of the bishop, could not make this election. The election of the Church is based on the election of God, and the election of God is discerned by many who are involved in the formation of the catechumens (see RCIA 121). The godparents are the primary ones who testify that the discernment has taken place and the catechumens are ready for this step.

The setting for the "Rite of Election" is the cathedral church, the presider is the diocesan bishop, the occasion is the First Sunday of Lent. Although exceptions are allowed for pastoral reasons, these are the norms against which any adaptations are measured. The lectionary readings for the First Sunday of Lent, particularly the Gospel of Jesus' temptations in the desert, give an eloquent witness to Jesus as the elect of God. His life-determining choices in the desert to live by God's word, to trust God humbly, and to worship God alone, are his yes to his election. Jesus is the model for all human faithfulness to God. The catechumens' yes is in him.

Baptized Candidates: What's Different?

Baptized candidates take part either in the "Rite of Calling the Candidates to Continuing Conversion" (RCIA 446), which is normally celebrated in the parish, with the pastor as its presider (RCIA 448) or the combined "Rite of Election and Call to Continuing Conversion" (RCIA 547 ff.) if they are a part of a mixed group of catechumens and candidates. The candidates do not sign the Book of the Elect.

As Lent begins, pastoral ministers must begin to look ahead to the celebration of the initiation sacraments at Easter. The priest who presides at the "Rite of Reception into the Full Communion of the Catholic Church" receives from the law itself the faculty to confirm such candidates. In the case of baptized Catholic candidates, however, a priest will need to receive from the bishop the faculty to confirm these candidates at the Easter Vigil, in accordance with RCIA 409. Permission should be sought according to the procedures of the local diocese.

What About Children?

The U.S. edition of the Rite offers an optional "Rite of Election" for children (RCIA 277 ff.). This rite is very similar to the rite for adults, with the exception that a special recognition of the godparents is scripted which concludes with a blessing for the parents and the godparents. If children are included with adults, the adult rite is followed (RCIA 279).

Music

For music notes and suggestions, see the section of this book on the "Rite of Sending" (p. 37).

Homily Suggestions

The gathering of a diverse group of catechumens and candidates with their sponsors at the cathedral church with the bishop at this juncture in the initiation process tempts the homilist to use as a focus either the assembly itself or the person of the bishop. Consider, instead, what is being celebrated at this rite: the election by God of God's people. In other words, the strongest consideration should be given in the homily to focusing not on ourselves but primarily upon the action of God in choosing us, in graciously identifying us as God's people.

This is not to imply that the gathering of diverse catechumens and candidates cannot be referred to within the homily. Nor does it mean that the bishop cannot express his own joy in meeting them. It simply means that the focus of the homily ought to be precisely where the Scriptures take us. While great latitude is given in the rite for selecting Scriptures (see RCIA 128), the first presumption is that one of the sets for the First Sunday of Lent would be used. Each of the three years of the cycle hone in on God's amazing grace in choosing a people, calling them his own, and in Christ, electing us for a life of witness in this world and, later, for a life on high around the heavenly throne. The forty days

of Jesus in the desert, his fasting and temptation, allude to the forty years of Israel in the desert. Where Israel failed, Jesus succeeds.

Christ is the elect of God; and we, the Church, his Body, are elected, favored and chosen by the One who will not let us go down into the dust. The Lord who loves us so much, that time and time again, divine initiative is taken to save us and set us free. How can we not celebrate our enrollment into the "book of life" (Revelation 3:5) and our name as "God's beloved"? How can we not, as a Church, rejoice with these catechumens and candidates and give them a good example as we accompany them along the path of the paschal mystery?

Decisions That Need To Be Made

- ✧ Diocesan liturgy brings together many different communities with various worship styles, musical repertoire, and cultural assumptions. Bringing together diverse groups of people can be an occasion of rich sharing, or confusion and dissatisfaction. One decision that needs to be made is who will prepare the liturgy. Will the goal be to represent a variety of groups, or to achieve a consistency of style?

- ✧ Who will evaluate the liturgy, and how will it be evaluated? Is there a mechanism in place for inviting the feedback of parish catechumenate groups and for sharing feedback with the ministers of the liturgy (particularly the bishop, the director of liturgy and the director of music)? Has time been set aside for a fresh reading of the ritual text each year, or have the adaptations of past years been continued without question?

- ✧ Practical questions must be addressed of how many and what kind of rites will be used. Many dioceses use the combined rite. A few have opted for separate rites for the baptized and the unbaptized. Numbers and geographical considerations have prompted multiple celebrations and locations.

- ✧ How will the community keep its focus on the theological meaning of the rite? Election is not a time for lessons about the bishop's chair, ring, miter, and crozier; it is not a time to shake the bishop's hand and receive his photograph. Planners must be vigilant about resisting such distractions.

The Scrutinies

A. Overview of the Rite

The Rite at a Glance

LITURGY OF THE WORD

- ✧ Readings
- ✧ Homily
- ✧ Invitation to Silent Prayer
- ✧ Intercessions for the Elect
- ✧ Exorcism
- ✧ Dismissal of the Elect

LITURGY OF THE EUCHARIST

Understanding the Rite

The meaning of the scrutinies is indicated in paragraphs 141–146 of the *Rite of Christian Initiation of Adults.* What is summarized there is a theology of prayer for healing and deliverance from evil that is rooted in the ancient baptismal tradition of the Church. These rites are "for self-searching and repentance and have above all a spiritual purpose. The scrutinies are meant to uncover, then heal all that is weak, defective, or sinful in the hearts of the elect; to bring out, then strengthen all that is upright, strong, and good. [They] are celebrated in order to deliver the elect from the power of sin and Satan, to protect them against temptation, and to give them strength in Christ. . . ." (RCIA 141). There are three scrutinies celebrated on the third, fourth, and fifth Sundays of Lent. By celebrating all three, the elect "progress in their perception of sin and their desire for salvation" (RCIA 143). It would be hard to overstate the importance of these rites for the

success of the period of purification and enlightenment, since they are meant to "complete the conversion of the elect and deepen their resolve to hold fast to Christ and to carry out their decision to love God above all" (RCIA 141).

The ritual requires that whenever the scrutinies are celebrated, the **readings** be taken from Year A of the Lectionary. This is because Year A contains the three great Johannine gospel texts of the woman at the well, the man born blind, and the raising of Lazarus that were used so often in the early centuries of the Church to prepare catechumens for Baptism. Each week's exorcism prayer (and the alternative form of the intercessions) uses the appropriate imagery of water, light/sight, or resurrection from the assigned gospel of that week. Some have complained that use of the Year A readings each year deprives congregations of the benefit of the wonderful readings found in Year B and Year C. However, there are many important passages of Scripture that the faithful never hear proclaimed in the Sunday liturgy, and the strong tradition behind the use of the Johannine texts at this time is so substantial that replacing them with Year B or Year C readings and adapting the exorcism prayers seems quite inadvisable.

The **homily** should prepare both the assembly and those for whom the scrutinies are celebrated to enter into the ritual with understanding and great fervor. In some communities this will require incorporating into the homily an explanation of what the scrutinies are and how they fit in the catechumenal journey. The Johannine pericopes, each in its own way, are stories of the search for faith—a search that ultimately leads to the discovery that Jesus alone is living water, light of the world, and life unending. The homilist's task is to unpack these readings in the context of the ongoing life experience of the local community, and to do so in such a way that his hearers are invited to deepen their faith in Jesus and to renew their commitment to faithful discipleship.

Since the scrutinies are very much about the Church's efficacious prayer for deliverance from evil, the homilist will also want to address how our world would seduce those preparing for initiation (and all of us!) with vain desires, moral blindness, and deadly sin. The fact that the scrutinies are public rituals, the prayer of the whole Body of Christ, also presents an excellent opportunity for the homilist to help Catholics move away from a privatistic and individualistic perspective and better understand the public, communal dimension of faith.

It might help the homilist to know that the group that worked on the development of the scrutiny ritual after the Second Vatican Council identified specific themes they wished to highlight in each of the scrutinies as a way to support the progressive nature of the scrutinies. In the "First Scrutiny," the thematic focus is on the mystery of personal sin; in the "Second Scrutiny," social sin; and in the "Third Scrutiny," the radical nature of sin as bringing ultimate death. One must be careful not to overstate this sequential movement, as some commentators have done, by saying that the "First Scrutiny" *is* about personal sin; the "Second Scrutiny," about social sin; and so forth. The Scriptures and the prayers of each of the scrutiny Sundays are, in fact, much too rich and multifaceted to be limited to a single thematic focus. However, it is helpful to remember these three dimensions of the mystery of sin and evil and to recognize how a particular Sunday's celebration might lend itself to emphasis on one aspect more than another. This is also a good reminder to homilists to think broadly about the task of preaching conversion and to realize how the coherence of the entire Lenten season offers an opportunity to preach in a way that leads the community progressively deeper into God's call to holiness of life.

The structure of the rite indicates that following the homily and once the elect have been called forward, the presider makes an **invitation to silent prayer,** first to the assembly and then to the elect themselves. This segment of the ritual has been given its own heading in the overall structure of the rite, and that fact tips us off to its importance. What is being asked for here is deep, substantial prayer—not the perfunctory three-second pause before getting on with the real stuff! The invitation must be powerful and convincing enough (though brief!) to signal to everyone concerned that they must turn to God with earnest hearts and focused attention. Once silence has fallen over the assembly, the presider should let it go on long enough to allow for significant prayer to happen. How long is "long enough"? A good rule of thumb is that the silence should last as long as possible and be ended just before restlessness sets in and begins to break the focus of the assembly. In communities not well schooled in silent prayer, that may be a matter of seconds; in communities more mature in the ways of prayer, the silence could easily last well over a full minute.

The **intercessions** come next. In our biblical and liturgical tradition of exorcistic prayer, the naming of evil holds an important place. To know the name of a demon or a deity was thought to give one a certain claim on its power, a control over its being, as is clear from the story of Jacob wrestling with the mysterious stranger (Genesis 32:23–32). This belief is also illustrated by the story in Genesis 2:19–20 in which God gives humans the right to name the animals, thus signaling that humans are being given dominion over them. Those who put together the *Rite of Christian Initiation of Adults* following the Second Vatican Council revised the format of the exorcism prayer in a significant way. Formerly, such prayers were addressed directly to the devil, as if the "evil one" (Matthew 13:19) were personally present in the person being prayed over. In the contemporary ritual, exorcistic prayer is addressed to God, asking that the one being exorcised be delivered or protected from the grasp of evil. Yet, it seems that in order not to lose the importance of naming evil directly, the current ritual inserts solemn intercessions just before the exorcism is prayed.

The ritual provides two examples of these intercessions in each of the scrutinies, with the second example always using imagery from the appropriate gospel text of the day. But the rubrics add that the intercessions "may be adapted to fit various circumstances" (RCIA 153). This provision should be taken as an invitation to make the intercessions real in the lives of the local community, to use them to name the evils with which the elect and the rest of the assembly are currently struggling. The more the content of the intercessions resonates with the lived experience of those present, the more will the naming of evil happen effectively and in the way that tradition has shown is so important for successful exorcistic prayer. The rubrics also indicate that if the general intercessions of the Mass are to be omitted, then intentions for the Church and world should be added here as well. Just as important as their content, of course, is the manner in which the intercessions are prayed. Suggestions for that proclamation are offered below, but suffice it to say here that great solemnity, vigor, and power should characterize the way that the Church names the evils from which we seek deliverance.

The prayer of **exorcism** is the heart of the scrutiny ritual. The rite's introduction ascribes remarkable potency to this prayer: "In the rite of exorcism . . . the elect . . . are freed from the effects of sin and from the influence of the devil. They receive new strength in the midst of their spiritual journey and they open their hearts to receive the gifts of the Savior" (RCIA 144). Given this high expectation of the exorcism, it is important to understand exactly how these prayers are structured and how they might best be prayed. All of the prayers have the same "shape," and only the language and imagery changes from week to week. First, there is an **invocation of God the Father** in which some aspect of God's saving power is remembered. This follows the familiar

Judeo-Christian formula of calling to mind God's saving history in the past before asking for specific grace in the present. After this opening invocation, a series of imperatives then make very focused demands on God's mercy by using words such as "protect," "defend," "free," "rescue," and so forth.

Following this prayer there is an optional imposition of hands that functions as a **silent invocation of the Holy Spirit.** It is difficult to imagine leaving out this important gesture, since its omission would destroy the implicit Trinitarian structure of the exorcism prayer. In addition, the evocative nature of a relatively prolonged silence in the assembly, accompanied by the presider's loving touch, makes the omission of this gesture a tragic impoverishment of the ritual. It must be noted, however, that what is asked for here is not just a perfunctory pat on the head. Rather, the prayer calls for laying hands firmly on each of the elects' heads and remaining fixed in deep, silent prayer for a substantial period of time.

The concluding segment of the exorcism prayer is an **address to Christ** as "Fountain," "Master," and "Holy One of God" (RCIA 154). The imagery of this part of the exorcism prayers is exceedingly rich and is a wonderful reminder of the christological nature of the entire conversion experience. It is Jesus Christ alone who is our Savior, and it is by virtue of his power as Lord that evil in all its forms has been overcome. These texts deserve to be proclaimed lovingly, strongly, and with a richness in style that befits their content. We will say more below about how that proclamation might happen most effectively.

After the exorcism prayer is completed, the rite provides the **option of singing a psalm or hymn.** The decision that is made here is crucial, lest the flow of the ritual that has built to this point be derailed or overwhelmed. Just the right selection of music must be made, if there is to be any singing here at all. The music can shift the mood slightly as a transitional element; or it may underscore even more deeply the mood already established, if that is what is desired. Those who decide about the use of this optional element should be very thoughtful as to what they want to achieve here and how best to do so.

The rite concludes with the usual **dismissal** of the elect to a catechetical session. For most communities, this is a routine element of the Sunday Eucharist. Regrettably, in some places the dismissal still happens only during Lent. If this is the case, particular attention must be made to see to it that the dismissal is experienced as a graceful procession (accompanied by appropriate music) rather than just an abrupt end or awkward exit. For communities still not practicing the dismissal on a regular basis, it might be helpful to note that the rubrics indicate that omission of the dismissal rite happens only "if for serious reasons the elect cannot leave" (RCIA 155).

Baptized Candidates: What's Different?

The adaptation of the *Rite of Christian Initiation of Adults* approved for use in the United States contains parallel rituals for baptized but uncatechized candidates. Despite strong injunctions in the "National Statutes for the Catechumenate" never to confuse the baptized with the unbaptized (RCIA, NS 2, 30–31), the rites adapted for them are in fact quite similar. At the first step of "Acceptance into the Order of Catechumens," for example, the two groups receive almost identical treatment. Celebrations of the Word, which are the linchpin of the catechumenate period, apply equally to baptized and unbaptized. Aside from occasions when certain of the minor rites are celebrated (such as "Anointing with the Oil of Catechumens"), one would be hard pressed in the early stages of the process to pick out of the catechumenate group just who is preparing for Baptism and who is not.

As the initiation process nears its culmination in the Easter sacraments, however, the differences between the two groups become more visible and pronounced in the liturgy. It is striking, for example, that at the outset of Lent the unbaptized sign the Book of the Elect but the baptized do not. Something is different here, the ritual action suggests. The conversion journeys of the unbaptized and the baptized are parallel, but they are not the same. The act of reserving the three scrutinies for the unbaptized alone, and celebrating for the baptized a single "Penitential Rite (Scrutiny)" is a continuation of this development.

The structure of the "Penitential Rite (Scrutiny)" is identical to that of the scrutiny, and further confusion arises because it is subtitled "(Scrutiny)" in the ritual text—a strange thing to do if the desired outcome is to maintain a sense of distinction. Yet a close look at the language of the scrutinies and the "Penitential Rite (Scrutiny)" reveals that their underlying theology is in fact quite different. The characteristic themes of rescue and deliverance from the powers of darkness that one finds in the texts of the scrutinies are absent from the "Penitential Rite (Scrutiny)." The language of the scrutinies is pastoral—there is some overlap here—yet there is always an edge and an urgency to the scrutinies, a sense that matters of life and death hang in the balance. This emphasis is consistent with the texts of the baptismal liturgy itself: the litany of saints, blessing of water, renunciations and promises. The milder language of the "Penitential Rite (Scrutiny)," on the other hand, evokes baptismal grace that the candidates already possess. Spiritual growth and healing—motifs familiar from the sacrament of Penance—give the "Penitential Rite (Scrutiny)" its characteristic tone.

The liturgy proposes that the assembly revisit the radical spiritual issues raised by the scrutinies three times each Lent in order to remember at the most basic level who we are and to whom we belong. In this strategic decision, the liturgy expresses a value judgment about the central and irreducible importance of Baptism. All of the baptized, including the baptized candidates, are called to engage with these issues by praying in the scrutinies with, for, and over the elect. In contrast, the baptized candidates in the present ritual may claim the solemn prayer of the assembly for their purification only once—not because they sin less often or less seriously than the unbaptized or because the initiation process is easier for them (although it may be), but because the symbolic center and axis on which the Lenten season turns is not reception into full communion, or completion of Christian initiation, but is Baptism.

The baptized candidates have recourse to the sacrament of Penance as the normal communal expression of purification within the community of the baptized. If the parish experience of the sacrament of Penance is anemic or lacks the communal dimension so important to ongoing conversion, the needs of the baptized candidates may be a spur to the renewal of the parish's penitential practices. The rite urges that penitential services be arranged for the baptized but uncatechized candidates to prepare them for the sacrament of Penance (RCIA 408). The Canadian edition of the *Rite of Christian Initiation of Adults* specifically suggests for the baptized candidates a liberal use of penitential celebrations found in Appendix II of the "Rite of Penance." While the American "Penitential Rite (Scrutiny)" for baptized candidates may be used in the Sunday assembly on the Second Sunday of Lent, it may also be used at another time when the community gathers. A gathering for a communal celebration of the sacrament of Penance may be one such opportunity. The freedom to adapt the texts of the rite (see RCIA 478) can be used to further enhance its appropriateness for the baptized candidates.

Pastoral leaders have disagreed about the wisdom of reserving the scrutinies for the unbaptized and creating a parallel "Penitential Rite (Scrutiny)" for the baptized. The pastoral benefit of repetition in the scrutinies and the strong language for describing the phenomenon of sin and its hold on humanity recommend the scrutiny as preferable to the "Penitential Rite (Scrutiny)" for those undergoing conversion, they feel, even when that conversion occurs after Baptism. Ambivalence in the ritual text itself— calling the "Penitential Rite (Scrutiny)" a scrutiny—suggests that baptized persons are indeed fit subjects of scrutinies, despite the decision to create a separate rite. Use has been made of the remarkable freedom given in paragraphs 478 and 407 to adapt catechumenal rites for the baptized. As a result some communities have created combined rites of scrutiny for both baptized and unbaptized, perhaps visibly separating the two groups to keep them distinct but using one set of adapted prayer texts for all. Further experience with the implementation of the U.S.

adaptations of the *Rite of Christian Initiation of Adults* will require continued critical reflection on both our pastoral practice and the theology of the rite. In the meanwhile, liturgical planners need to take into account the following points when deciding how to minister to the baptized candidates:

- ✧ the pastoral purposes of the rite,
- ✧ the needs of the local assembly,
- ✧ the theology of the rite,
- ✧ the principle of respect for Baptism, and
- ✧ the ritual structure of the Lenten season.

What About Children?

In the *Rite of Christian Initiation of Adults,* the chapter adapted for children of catechetical age (RCIA 291ff.) considers the celebration of the scrutiny to be "the second step in the children's Christian initiation" (the first being the "Rite of Acceptance"). The U. S. edition of the ritual has recognized a serious omission and added an optional "Rite of Election" prior to the scrutiny. However, there remain a number of elements of the children's "Penitential Rite (Scrutiny)" that raise pastoral concerns about its appropriateness and effectiveness.

The "Penitential Rite (Scrutiny)" for children contains the awkward proposal that the celebration of First Penance for the baptized children of the parish be combined with this celebration. In addition, the structure of the children's celebration departs from the normative adult version in significant ways. Most striking is the adapted shape of the prayer of exorcism. Instead of the Trinitarian structure followed in all of the adult exorcism prayers, there are two examples provided neither of which is Trinitarian in nature. The exorcisms are quite brief and lack the vigor of the adult prayers. Furthermore, they lack any allusion to accompanying scriptural texts that—by way of reference—could have provided more substance. By comparison to the robust adult prayers for deliverance from evil, the children's texts seem quite anemic. After the exorcism prayer, there is the option of anointing the elect with the oil of catechumens or laying hands on them. If the latter option is chosen, there is an address to the children that precedes the silent laying on of hands. Then the children are either dismissed or sent back to their seats while First Penance is celebrated for the other children.

The rite contains a remarkable permission (RCIA 294) for the local community to create an entire second scrutiny for children. One does not know whether to applaud the trust this shows in local liturgical teams or to lament an attitude of indifference to rites for children that are purportedly "major occasions in their catechumenate" (RCIA 291). What seems clear is that the adult ritual offers a superior model and easily incorporates children into its celebration. The best pastoral option, it seems, would be to exercise the permission of adapting by simply including children along with adults in a single celebration that follows the normative adult rite.

Scheduling the Scrutinies

The normal time for the celebration of the scrutinies is during the celebration of the Eucharist on the third, fourth, and fifth Sundays of Lent. In the U. S. edition of the *Rite of Christian Initiation of Adults,* the "Penitential Rite (Scrutiny)" for baptized candidates is designated for the Second Sunday of Lent. Although these times are normative, it is clear that pastoral realities must always be taken into consideration, and the rite itself recognizes that flexibility may be needed. In the "Introduction" (RCIA 20) there is even mention of the possibility of celebrating the scrutinies on "convenient weekdays," and the scrutinies themselves envision the possibility of a celebration that does not include a Liturgy of the Eucharist. The "Introduction" (RCIA 20) also recognizes the possibility of "serious reasons" or "extraordinary circumstances" that might require the celebration of only one or two scrutinies instead of the usual three. In the adaptation for children of catechetical age, only one scrutiny (also called a penitential rite) is provided that is foreseen as a Lenten celebration, but a specific time is not indicated. The rubrics suggest a second scrutiny should be celebrated with children, again during the Lenten season, but great freedom is provided in a rubric (RCIA 294) that allows the local community to compose the texts of that celebration and to decide when it occurs.

Despite this flexibility, pastoral practice in the United States has indicated the high value of celebrating all of the scrutinies during the Sunday Eucharist on the three traditional Sundays. Experience has also shown that children of catechetical age do not need to follow the "watered down" suggestion of the rite that only one or two scrutinies be held for them. Very few communities have even attempted to implement the strange suggestion that the scrutiny for children might also be combined with the celebration of First Penance by a peer group of baptized children of the parish. Instead, children in the catechumenate seem to do very well participating in the adult ritual for all three weeks.

Since the celebration of the scrutinies has great value for the entire community, not just for the elect, it is desirable that as many members of the community as possible be able to participate in these important rituals. In some parishes it will be possible to have a few members of the catechumenate at each of the Sunday Masses on all three designated Sundays. In other places, only one or two Masses may be designated for the scrutiny on each of the three weeks. While each community will have to decide for itself, the general principle to be followed in setting the schedule should be to maximize the number of parishioners who are able to participate.

Catechetical and Spiritual Preparation of the Elect

The reader is referred to the *Resource Book for Purification and Enlightenment* that is part of the *Foundations in Faith* series. In Part One of that book, helpful tips are given regarding how to help the entire parish community experience the initiatory character of the Lenten season. Part Two, Chapter 5, also contains specific catechetical material that is designed to

prepare those most immediately involved in the scrutiny, as well as other members of the community who may be interested in joining the preparation session(s). While not repeated here, that material is an integral part of what must be said about how best to prepare the community for the scrutinies.

Preparing the Ministers

The structure of the scrutiny ritual is quite straightforward and simple. Nonetheless, a successful celebration will require that all of the ministers be carefully prepared for their respective parts. As with other celebrations, it is suggested that the rehearsal not include the elect themselves. Instead the **godparent** should be carefully rehearsed and be comfortable with the flow of the rite and able to guide his or her charge with confidence throughout the ritual. During the rehearsal, the godparent should be reminded about the importance of keeping the right hand constantly on the shoulder of the elect. The rubrics direct this gesture only during the intercessions, but it seems preferable that it be held throughout. This reassuring touch deepens in significance as the assembly and the elect come to understand more and more deeply the godparent's important role as guide and protector. The air of confidence that the godparent radiates during the rite is an important expression of the way that mother Church cares for those who are young and tender in the ways of faith.

The **presider,** of course, plays a crucial part in this ritual. There are several places where he must make remarks that are not scripted in the rite but that are very important for keeping the focus and the flow of the rite on target. The first is during the invitation to silent prayer, which is addressed initially to the assembly and then to the elect. Next there is the introduction to the intercessions, and at the end he offers words of dismissal. At each of these points, well-chosen words will help to open up the meaning of the rite for all in attendance. Unless he is extraordinarily gifted at *ex tempore* speech, the presider should give careful thought beforehand to just what he will say and how best to express it, so that the value of these few opportunities is not lost. The presence of the presider at the rehearsal is important, since there needs to be clear understanding between him and the godparents about positions, movements, cues, and so forth.

In some communities the **director** or **coordinator** of the catechumenate assists the presider throughout the ritual as a way of highlighting the important role that he or she plays in the process. Standing by the presider's side, calling forth the elect at the proper time, perhaps assisting with the presider's book,

joining in the laying on of hands—these are some of the ways that the director or coordinator can participate in the ritual in a meaningful way.

The place of music in the rite is rather underdeveloped. The sole indication concerning music that is offered in the official text is for an optional song after the prayer of exorcism. Some suggestions are given here about how the musical component can be developed. Depending on how this happens, the role of **ministers of music** will vary. One of the musicians may be involved in the composition of the intercessions and setting them to music. A cantor-accompanist team may need to prepare the proclamation of the intercessions and other musical elements (they should be clear about their cues and how what they are doing fits into the overall movement of the rite). Music needs to be selected and provided for the assembly, and, of course, it is important that the assembly knows its sung parts and be as carefully rehearsed as the choir or other music ministers are.

Since the scrutiny will normally be celebrated at a Sunday Eucharist, there will be a number of **other liturgical ministers** who are affected by this celebration. Ushers/greeters should be alerted to the implications of the rite for them. They may have extra hospitality duties, be involved in directing participants to their places, or be responsible for distributing special participation aids to the assembly. The servers should be at the rehearsal and very familiar with the entire ritual and their part in it. Lectors may have their routine adjusted, depending on whether the general intercessions are combined with the litany. They should know what is happening and how it will affect them. If there should be a deacon or master of ceremonies, these ministers also need to be "in the loop" with what is happening so that they can support rather than detract from the ritual action. Clearly, there needs to be someone from the liturgy committee/planners or the catechumenate team who can oversee and coordinate all of the elements of the rite so that everything comes together smoothly. The scrutiny is deceptively simple in appearance—all the more reason why it must be carefully prepared and executed if it is to deliver the "punch" that it is meant to have.

Engaging the Assembly

Scheduling the celebration of the scrutinies so that as many as possible may participate is the most basic step that must be taken. But more must be done to facilitate the "full, conscious and active participation of all the faithful" (*Constitution on the Sacred Liturgy* 14) in the celebration, which is the aim of true liturgical renewal. Special efforts must be made to connect the "ordinary parishioner" to the very powerful realities that are involved in the Church's celebration of the scrutinies.

Catechumenate team members may want to brainstorm ways to attract various groups to participate with the elect in the kind of preparation session described in the *Resource Book for Purification and Enlightenment,* pp. 111ff. These sessions are ideal ways for small faith communities, youth ministry Confirmation groups, members of the ladies' sodality or men's club, and so forth to get to know better and to offer support to those in the catechumenate. The members of the adult choir in one parish chose to hold a retreat day for themselves during Lent that was modeled on preparation of the elect for the scrutinies. After a day of prayer, reflection, and sharing around the evils from which they sought deliverance, the music ministers celebrated a prayer for healing modeled closely on the scrutinies.

Catechists in the parish's religious education program and youth ministry should be well informed about the scrutinies and encouraged to incorporate into their Lenten formation efforts some time devoted to preparing for the celebration of the scrutinies. The focus of their efforts might well include topics such as the history of Lent and the role the scrutinies played in its development (see *Resource Book for Purification and Enlightenment,* pp. 9–26), the Church's tradition of exorcistic prayer and how it is to be understood today, an exercise to name the demonic forces operative in our contemporary world, and the importance of the larger community's involvement in the faith journey of those preparing for Christian initiation. As preparations are made for the parish's Lenten communal celebration of the sacrament of Penance, the liturgy team might be invited to think in terms of how insights from the catechumenal process might be applicable to parishioners at large. Catechesis preparing for the communal celebration of Penance could be focused on naming the evils we find in ourselves, in our Church, and in society. And certain elements of the Penance service (e.g., the confession of sins) could be developed along lines similar to the scrutiny (e.g., the litany before the exorcism).

Sample Bulletin Announcement/Background (Second Sunday of Lent) for the scrutinies

Next weekend at the *(times)* Masses we will celebrate the "First Scrutiny" for those in our catechumenal process who are preparing for initiation at the Easter Vigil. The following week, at the *(times)* Masses, we will celebrate the "Second Scrutiny," and on *(dates and times)* Masses, the "Third Scrutiny."

The scrutinies are also called by the more exotic name "major exorcisms." As such, they are among the most ancient prayers in the Christian liturgical tradition. As early as the second century, Christian communities would help those who had been chosen for Baptism to prepare for their initiation by laying on hands and by prayers for protection and deliverance from evil (i.e., exorcisms). At the beginning of the third century, Hippolytus told the Christians at Rome to celebrate these rites with catechumens on a daily basis during the final stages of preparation for Baptism.

Today we continue to celebrate these powerful rituals, convinced that those about to enter into a covenant with God in Christ stand in need of our prayers for deliverance and protection. We also understand today that our prayers for protection from evil are not limited to those formally engaged in the catechumenal process. Just as our entire community is called to journey with the catechumens throughout the Lenten season, we recognize the need we all share for freedom from evil and its effects.

That is why for the next three weeks we will use the Lectionary's "scrutiny readings" from Year A at all Masses, even when there is no scrutiny at a particular celebration. This week at a special gathering of those in preparation for Confirmation, as well as those in our catechumenal community, we ask their help in naming the evils from which we must seek God's deliverance and protection. We urge you to prepare for the celebration of the scrutinies in a personal way by discerning what it is in your own life that needs to be freed from sin's bondage. Join in spirit with all in our community who turn to Jesus for freedom from sin and protection from all evil.

Sample Pulpit Announcement the Week Before the Rite

Next week at the *(times)* Masses, we will celebrate the *"(number)* Scrutiny" with those in our catechumenate. These very moving and powerful prayers ask God's protection on those who will soon become full members of our Catholic Church through the sacraments of Baptism, Confirmation, and Eucharist. In the scrutinies, we pray for deliverance from evil and protection against all of the demonic forces that would enslave the disciples of Jesus. Your prayers and your support are important for our sisters and brothers who have been journeying for so many months toward the sacraments of Christian initiation. Please join us next week, and please continue to hold in your Lenten prayers the elect who count on you for support in making their faith journey.

Environment

What has been said above about restraint and sobriety certainly applies to the environment of the worship space throughout the season of Lent. Very likely nothing extra needs to be done on the three scrutiny Sundays by way of decoration. However, a tasteful way of highlighting the three themes of the Johannine readings could give the assembly a sense of the progressive movement of the scrutinies. If this is to be done, planners should avoid a one-dimensional approach that tends to be merely literal and representational, as sometimes happens when there is a table with a water jug one week, a candle the next, and burial wrappings the next. That kind of "display art" does little to engage the imagination of the assembly. Better to do nothing than to hit people over the head with the "message" that the planners think is supposed to be conveyed.

The major environmental concern on these Sundays should be how best to allow the assembly to experience the power of the ritual action. Visibility and proximity of the elect to the assembly is much more important than placing different gospel-related images around the worship space. Careful thought should be given to the location of each "station" where the elect will stand and kneel during the rite. The movement of the presider from one elect to another elect during the laying on of hands must flow smoothly. This must be taken into consideration when arranging the overall layout of the rite.

Some communities have also experimented with placing other ministers (lectors, cantors) at strategic places throughout the assembly during the proclamation of the Gospel (if it is read in parts) or during the litany. Decisions to change familiar locations for such proclamations signal "something special is happening." But this is tricky business, and it must be very carefully done to avoid a feeling of gimmickry. Nonetheless, such arrangements if not overused, can certainly convey "the message" of what is being proclaimed with fresh power and immediacy. Another possibility to enhance the environment is judicious use of incense. A simple brazier with a few grains of incense wordlessly applied as the scrutiny begins can be a powerfully evocative symbol of how our prayers rise heavenward during this most solemn ritual.

Music

Here are some places where music can be used in this rite:

- ✧ Given the length of the scrutiny gospel readings, acclamations by the people, inserted at strategic points in the gospel reading, can be an excellent way of maintaining the assembly's attention and focus. Underscoring the entire Gospel also works well to support and lead into the people's acclamations.

- ✧ Chanting the entire gospel reading works if it is done well by a deacon or priest with a trained voice.

- ✧ A cantor may chant the litany, with sung assembly responses.

- ✧ The presider can chant the exorcism prayer.

- ✧ People's acclamations can be inserted into the exorcism prayer as a way of punctuating and highlighting the text.

- ✧ Musical underscoring can accompany a spoken proclamation of the exorcism prayer. (Note: if this is done, the underscoring should stop during the laying on of hands.)

- ✧ A song may be sung at the end of the exorcism prayer.

- ✧ Instrumental music or a sung refrain may be used as the elect are dismissed from the assembly.

Music Suggestions

The chanting of the litany of intercession can be a very powerful element in the ritual. Various communities have experimented with ways to proclaim the naming of evil that takes place in the litany in a way that gives the assembly a felt experience of the struggle between good and evil that characterizes the Christian journey. When the cantor's voice has a certain stridency, when the tempo gradually quickens with each succeeding set of invocations, when the volume builds with each evil that is named, a litany with "punch" results—one that evokes the reality of those demonic forces from which we seek deliverance.

As suggested, the acclamations by the assembly might be used to punctuate the exorcism prayer of the presider. If the acclamations have been incorporated in the gospel reading, those same refrains can be used again during the exorcism prayer.

Some appropriate musical selections might be:

Music for the Intercessions:
- ❖ "Litany of Deliverance" (Cooney, GIA Publications)
- ❖ Rite of Scrutinies: "I Heard the Voice of Jesus Say" (Haugen, GIA Publications)
- ❖ "Litany Acclamation" from *Who Calls You By Name* (Hass, GIA Publications)
- ❖ Chanted Intercession with Gregorian "Kyrie Eleison" Response
- ❖ "God of All Power," "God of All Mercy," "God of the Living" from *Who Calls You By Name* (Hass, GIA Publications)

Optional Song after Exorcism, Psalm or Hymn:
(Note: Psalm suggestions are found in RCIA 154, 168, and 175.)

First Scrutiny
- ❖ "I Am the Living Water" from *Music for Children's Liturgy of the Word* (Walker, OCP)
- ❖ "Water of Life" (Haas, GIA Publications)
- ❖ "The Water I Give" from *Who Calls You By Name* Vol. 1 (Haas, GIA Publications)
- ❖ "As Water to the Thirsty" (Haas, GIA Publications)
- ❖ "I Heard the Voice of Jesus Say" (tune: Kingsfold, GIA Publications)

Second Scrutiny
- ❖ "I Am the Light in Darkness" from *Music for Children's Liturgy of the Word* (Walker, OCP)
- ❖ "Jesus Christ, Inner Light" (Toolan, OCP)
- ❖ "Walk in the Light" (Landry, OCP)
- ❖ "Out of Darkness" (Walker, OCP)
- ❖ "He Healed the Darkness of My Mind" from *Who Calls You By Name* Vol. 1 (Haas, GIA Publications)
- ❖ "Amazing Grace"

Third Scrutiny
- ❖ "I Am the Resurrection" from *Music for Children's Liturgy of the Word* (Walker, OCP)
- ❖ "Christ Will Be Your Light" from *Who Calls You By Name* Vol. 1 (Haas, GIA Publications)
- ❖ "Awake, O Sleeper" (Haugen, GIA Publications)
- ❖ "I Am the Bread of Life" verses 4 and 5 (Toolan, GIA Publications)

Homily Suggestions

First Scrutiny

In preparing for this homily, the preacher, after praying over the Sunday Scriptures for Year A, may want to refresh his memory regarding the notes concerning the scrutiny celebrations (RCIA 141–146). In addition it would be useful to read over the specific exorcism prayers (especially RCIA 154 A and B) for their powerful images. Finally, the homilist will want to peruse the images found in the Sacramentary, in the opening prayer of the Mass and the proper preface for this day.

The Scriptures for the Third Sunday of Lent Year A revolve around Christ who provides for us living water. Note the headings, which help point out the major theme of each reading. The first reading, from Exodus, describes the longing of God's people for water to drink. This is a physical lack that they ask God to remedy. The Scriptures rapidly move beyond this physical deprivation to address deeper, more spiritual needs. The second reading, from Paul's Letter to the Romans, praises the love of God that has been poured into the hearts of believers through the action of the Holy Spirit. This gift, celebrated in the gospel pericope, ultimately leads us to contemplate the eternal life into which we are drawn by the generosity of Jesus.

There are many different and valid perspectives from which the homilist might preach this good news. For example, the homilist may want to focus on how God creates us humans with a capacity for thirst, a desire for the holy, the good—for God's very self. Or the homilist may want to focus on how the elect have encountered the love of Jesus in their initiation journey and have been invited by the Lord to drink of the waters of life he offers. Or the homilist may want to focus on how the Messiah courts us, how he thirsts for our faith just as much as he thirsted for the faith of the Samaritan woman at the well (see the Sacramentary, Preface P14) and awakens in all our hearts the fire of divine love.

In whatever way these Scriptures and this scrutiny celebration are approached homiletically, the good news of God's overwhelming love, his lavish grace, must be emphasized. This is a well that will not run dry. Water from above, heaven's gift, will drown us in depths of love. This flood of love makes of us a new creation and enables us to evangelize all our brothers and sisters. We will not be able to keep silent about this gift. Like a laughing brook, we will babble about the love that has changed us.

Whoever drinks the water God gives, discovers a spring inside, welling up for eternal life. We are watered in Christ so that whatever is weak may be strengthened, whatever is broken restored, whatever is lost found, and what is found redeemed.

Second Scrutiny

This Johannine gospel episode is so very rich that, even if the homilist and assembly were to reflect upon it year after year on the Fourth Sunday of Lent, new ideas for preaching would not be lacking. Although the image of Jesus as the light of the world leaps out from the scriptural page, any number of approaches to this image or implications drawn from it will suggest themselves.

In exploring the images and implications that arise from the gospel text and the other two Scriptures for this Sunday, the homilist may wish to reflect upon the preface from the Sacramentary (P 15) and the exorcism prayers from this "Second Scrutiny" (RCIA 168).

The homilist may also want to peruse a meaty commentary on this gospel passage, such as the one by Francis J. Moloney, SDB in the fourth volume of the *Sacra Pagina* series. This or a similar resource can provide fresh ways of seeing scriptural material that may have become dull because of familiarity. Remember, however, that no matter how the various commentaries open up this scriptural episode and its various scenes and characters, the heart of the good news is found in the encounter of a blind man with Jesus.

Because of his encounter with Jesus, however, the blind man receives the gift of sight. The light of faith drives the darkness of sin away. We are enlightened by the Christ, the Anointed One sent by God; the illuminating grace that he offers is a gift. We cannot achieve this illumination, this seeing, on our own. Yet a choice presents itself to us. We could remain in stubborn blindness, willfully rejecting the gift being offered, or we can accept the shining truth that transforms us into witnesses to the faith.

Third Scrutiny

This scrutiny and its scriptural texts are about life, an authentic life promised to us by God that even the grave cannot take away as it claims our mortal remains. This is about the effects of sin, deadly sin, that entomb us and this world. This is about a Savior who weeps for us because he does not come to condemn us but to redeem us. This is about the voice of Christ, who calls us forth into a life that triumphs over sin and death and Satan's pride. This is about love, divine love and how it names us as friends, brothers and sisters, a family of mercy and fullness.

The name of the Samaritan woman at the well is not recorded in the Gospel of John. Neither is the name of the man born blind who is given sight. The texts that provide the homiletic focus for the first and second scrutinies are undoubtedly powerful. But the particular gospel text of the raising of Lazarus has been saved for last. The Johannine community remembered Mary, Martha and Lazarus by name because Jesus loved them as dear friends.

Lazarus becomes an icon for each believer who is loved deeply by Christ. This saving love bids us come out from the tomb of sin and death. This saving love commands that all restraints holding us back from fullness of life be unbound. This saving love gives to the Church sacraments that lift us up to everlasting life.

Penitential Rite for Baptized Candidates

Given that the Rite (RCIA 461) suggests that the celebration of the "Penitential Rite" might help to prepare the candidates for sacramental Reconciliation, the following homily suggestions incorporate not only ideas building on the Second Sunday of Lent but also on the nature of Penance and Reconciliation.

In this mountaintop revelation Peter, James, and John are given a glimpse of the glory to come. They are dumfounded and bewildered. Yet they clearly are enthralled. The voice from heaven commands them to listen. To what must they listen?

They must listen, as must we, to the voice of the beloved child of God, Jesus, who teaches us the ways of holiness, the ways of the kingdom. This listening, on our part, requires humility—a surrender to the grace offered us in the truth and beauty of the Lord and the Lord's way of life.

Sometimes in that surrender to ultimate goodness, we discover that we do not measure up. At the same time, however, the Gospel assures us of the mercy of God who accords us the same status of Christ as beloved children. As children of God, we are healed and freed of sin. Redemption is ours if we but repent and believe in the Gospel.

This victory is brought to light in Baptism. Our fallen nature is crucified with Christ so that we might rise with him in glory—a glory first glimpsed by the disciples on the mountaintop of the Transfiguration. We rejoice that we can approach the Lord in sacramental Reconciliation and unburden ourselves of our sins, casting them aside in order to listen more closely to his voice, to follow and enter into the kingdom of glory.

The homilist will want to remind candidates that sacramental Reconciliation is joyful. The focus is not so much on our sins as it is on the healing power of Christ who redeems us. In other words, we are confessing God's intense love of us as much as we are confessing our sins.

The content of this preaching will also be much more accessible to the candidates if a narrative is shared stressing healing or the release from sinfulness. Stories are infinitely better than instruction—especially when it comes to the first-time celebration of Reconciliation.

Tips for Presiders

In a famous article early in the last century, a liturgical scholar by the name of Edmund Bishop characterized a number of the qualities that constituted the specific identity of the Roman rite. Sobriety in prayer texts and structure was one of the most important elements of style that Bishop argued is fundamental to the native "genius" of the Roman tradition. The penitential character of the entire Lenten season, of course, already invites us to a certain restraint. Even more so the scrutinies seem to call for that noble simplicity and sobriety of manner in which they are celebrated. Presiders need to keep this in mind as they set the mood for the entire celebration. Here are some thoughts:

✧ This is not the time for chatty humor during the opening rites of the Mass nor for adding "extras" to the day's liturgy. The focus should be placed relentlessly on the scrutinies and on God's action of purification and enlightenment through their celebration.

✧ Make certain that you meet with the elect both before and after the day's celebration. The intensity and intimacy of these rites can often stir up in the elect deep feelings and memories of their personal struggles with sin. They will look for your pastoral care as part of the healing process that the scrutinies are meant to accomplish.

✧ In the introductions and transitions that you must compose, it is important that you acknowledge the solidarity the rest of the assembly has with the elect for whom we are praying. Otherwise it might seem as if "we" are the holy ones praying for "them," the sinners. Remember also that too much verbiage will detract from, not add to, the sobriety of the rite. Less is more!

✧ Perhaps your single most important contribution to the effectiveness of the rite will be your body language and your sense of prayerful presence during the laying on of hands. Show that you are comfortable with profound silence by taking time for deep prayer with each of the elect. Remember that your firm but gentle touch is a channel for God's healing grace in the life of each person on whom you lay hands.

✧ Invite others to follow you in laying on of hands. Make certain that you have practiced with them beforehand, so that they also understand the impact of their body language in conveying the meaning of the rite.

How Will the Assembly Be Active and Involved?

Here are some thoughts:

✧ Make certain that in advance of the rite there are catechetical efforts that aim at engaging the assembly in a reflective process on how we experience the grasp of evil, and where it is that the local community most needs deliverance.

✧ See to it that the evils that are named as a result of this process find their way into the litany of intercession that will be prayed each week. Remind the community that this is happening—that they themselves have named what it is we are praying about.

✧ Planners should work closely with musicians (see p. 52) to identify how music can be a primary vehicle for facilitating the involvement of the assembly in the celebration. Make certain that the community knows the music it is expected to sing.

✧ Consider having the elect remain kneeling throughout the litany and the exorcism prayers. Invite the assembly to join them in this penitential posture during the litany as a way of expressing their solidarity with the elect in the need for God's protection and healing from sin. Remind the assembly that we not only pray *for* the elect; we pray *with* them for God's mercy!

✧ Instead of having all of the elect in the sanctuary at some distance from the assembly, consider spacing them in the aisles throughout the nave. Strive for a physical proximity to the entire assembly (even the folks in the last pew) that promotes an immediacy and engages everyone.

✧ During the laying on of hands, others besides the presider may be invited to join. The director and/or other members of the catechumenate team may be appropriate, as are sponsors, and sometimes even some members from the assembly might be invited to participate. However, there should not be so much movement that prayerful silence is disrupted.

❖ The singing of a psalm or hymn immediately at the conclusion of the last exorcism prayer can be an excellent way to allow the entire assembly to give voice to its feelings. This is especially true when the ritual has been a deeply moving one.

How Will We Highlight the Central Symbols?

Here are some ideas:

❖ Remember that the elect themselves are living symbols of God's grace at work in the community. The way that godparents lovingly guide them to their place for the prayers, and even their placement within the assembly, ought to bespeak the sacredness of their presence within our midst.

❖ The way in which the litany prayers and the exorcism prayers are proclaimed must make evident the power that we associate with naming evil and calling upon God to bind its harmful effects in our lives. These prayers must be prayed with majesty and with a seriousness of purpose that causes a hush to fall on the assembly. We offer some ideas (see p. 52) about how to use music to accomplish this. Even if all of the texts are spoken, special attention must be given to matters of pacing, inflection, and other elements of the spoken idiom so that all recognize the "special" character of these particular texts.

❖ Touch is a primal symbol in our liturgical tradition. See to it that the laying on of hands is not omitted and prolonged sufficiently to communicate deep prayer and loving concern. The presider may need to be helped in order to recognize how crucial his own body language is at this point in the ritual. He must not rush through this element in the rite if it is to be successful.

D. After the Rite

Evaluation of the Scrutinies/Penitential Rite

During the week following the celebration, set aside some time to evaluate the rite. The fact that there will be successive celebrations in a short period of time allows liturgical planners to make revisions and improvements for the next week. Make certain that the evaluation includes some of the elect and sponsors, as well as other key liturgical ministers and members of the assembly. Including as many viewpoints as possible will increase the value of the evaluation.

A process like this one may be helpful:

❖ Duplicate and distribute the reflection sheet on page 57 to those who will take part in the evaluation.

❖ Have the evaluators reflect on their experiences of the rite and fill out the sheet privately.

❖ Gather a group together to share what they have written and why. Out of this discussion, formulate specific suggestions for improvement.

❖ See to it that those responsible for the rite get sufficient feedback so that they understand the reasons behind the suggestions for improvement.

Evaluation: Rite of Scrutiny

The rite celebrated was: _____ "Penitential Rite (Scrutiny)"

_____ "Rite of Scrutiny for Baptized Candidates"

_____ Scrutiny

_____ Children's "Penitential Rite (Scrutiny)"

Date of celebration _____ Time of celebration _____

Number of elect _____   Number of candidates _____

1. For me the highlight of the rite was _____

   because _____ .

2. For me the part of the rite that was least meaningful was _____

   because _____ .

3. If I were to describe the important parts of this rite to others, I would tell them _____

   _____ .

4. Rate the following on a scale of 1–10 (1 is low, 10 is high) on how well

   this part of the rite was celebrated and give a reason for your response.

   _____ Proclamation of the Gospel _____

   _____ Homily _____

   _____ Presider's way of calling the elect forward and inviting all to silent prayer _____

   _____ Intercessions for the elect _____

   _____ Exorcism prayer _____

   _____ Laying on of hands _____

   _____ Song after the exorcism _____

   _____ Dismissal of the elect _____

   _____ Music used during the rite _____

5. If I were to change something in how this rite is celebrated the next time, I would suggest _____

   _____

   because _____ .

6. Other details that need to be remembered for the next celebration are: _____

   _____ .

Mystagogy

Just as mystagogy is a whole period of time for neophytes to reflect on their experience of the Easter sacraments, each celebration of a liturgical rite merits mystagogical reflection. Mystagogical reflection gives those who have celebrated a rite a further way to take in and deepen their experience. Fuller appreciation for the rite comes as words are given to an experience. Likewise, a time of mystagogy fosters a theological understanding of the rite. (Consult the *Mystagogia Resource Book* in the *Foundations in Faith* series for a fuller understanding of mystagogy.) In the scrutinies a deeper sense of sin, evil, and the power of God's deliverance is often unfolded. Minimally, those who have celebrated the rite should be given the opportunity for mystagogical reflection when they are dismissed. Others involved in the rite may also be able to participate in the extended reflection at a later time.

The reader is referred to the resource book for the period of purification and enlightenment that is part of the *Foundations in Faith* series. There mystagogical sessions are provided for the "Penitential Rite" on the Second Sunday of Lent (pp. 50–53) and for each of the three scrutinies on the third, fourth, and fifth Sundays of Lent (pp. 58–61, 70–73, 82–85).

Third Step: Celebration of the Sacraments of Initiation

A. Overview of the Rite

The Rite at a Glance

SERVICE OF LIGHT

LITURGY OF THE WORD

CELEBRATION OF BAPTISM

    Presentation of the Candidates

    Invitation to Prayer

    Litany of the Saints

    Prayer over the Water

    Profession of Faith

        Renunciation of Sin

        Profession of Faith

    Baptism

    Explanatory Rites

        [Clothing with a Baptismal Garment]

        Presentation of a Lighted Candle

CELEBRATION OF CONFIRMATION

    Invitation

    Laying on of Hands

    Anointing with Chrism

RENEWAL OF BAPTISMAL PROMISES

LITURGY OF THE EUCHARIST

Understanding the Rite

In the Easter Vigil the sacraments of **Baptism** and **Confirmation** are celebrated, and the whole initiatory process reaches its high point in the celebration of the **Eucharist,** which the neophytes share in for the first time. The initiation sacraments are integrated into a magnificent liturgy that stands at the center of the whole liturgical year and is arguably the most beautiful liturgy the Church has in its power to celebrate. The Easter Vigil celebrates the **paschal mystery**—the dying and rising of Jesus Christ—and the participation in the paschal mystery by God's faithful people. What happens to the elect in this liturgy brings into powerful focus the paschal character of the celebration for the entire assembly.

The Easter Vigil may be roughly divided into four parts: the Service of Light, the Liturgy of the Word, the Liturgy of Baptism, and Confirmation, and the Liturgy of the Eucharist. All parts of the Vigil contribute to the celebration of the sacraments of initiation and must be celebrated fully and well. The **Service of Light,** for example, proclaims the whole Easter mystery, from creation through redemption. A roaring fire, a splendid paschal candle, a reverent and spirited procession of the people with the candle into the church, and the magnificent text of the Exsultet sung with passion are its essential elements. In a similar way, the **Liturgy of the Word,** with its seven Old Testament readings pivoting on the crossing of the Red Sea from the book of Exodus, allows the story of salvation to unfold through the Law and the Prophets. The Liturgy of the Word proclaims the work of God in creation and redemption, a work which is about to be experienced anew in the sacrament of Baptism. At every juncture in the Liturgy of the Word, the elect and the assembly hear in the biblical story, their own story, and most especially on this night, they hear in the paschal story their own calling out of death and into new life.

There can be no question of paring down these earlier parts of the liturgy to save time for the rituals of initiation. A vigil, by its nature, requires time to do its work. If rushed, it ceases to be a vigil. At various times in history the events of the Easter Vigil were in fact cued by the cosmos: "at cockcrow" Baptisms could begin, or "when the first star appeared in the sky" the fire could be lit. The assembly waited upon the heavens. One vestige of this sensibility still exists in the contemporary requirement to begin the Vigil after nightfall. Even beyond such specific directives, the quality of the Vigil is always one of gradual unfolding. The pace picks up with the initiation sequence that follows the Liturgy of the Word, but the earlier parts are as stately and unhurried as the planets on their courses.

The rites of initiation begin with the **presentation of the candidates** for Baptism and an **invitation to prayer.** The **litany of the saints,** which then follows, can accompany the procession to the font, or it can be sung at the font if no procession is needed. This litany calls on all the saints to pray for us and signals the great importance of what is to take place. By invoking the saints at this point, the liturgy shows that the Church in heaven and on earth is gathered at the font, interceding for those about to be baptized. The **blessing of the water** employs rich imagery to recall the place of water in all saving history and culminates in calling down the Holy Spirit upon the water of the font right now. The gesture of plunging the paschal candle into the water suggests that Christ himself makes the water fertile, so that new life can come forth from this font. Sung acclamations increase the involvement of the assembly in this prayer of blessing.

The drama of faith's decision is acted out vividly in the **renunciation of sin** and the **profession of faith** of the elect. While the renunciation may be done as a group, the profession of faith always takes place individually. Then each candidate for **Baptism** either is immersed or water is poured on him or her as the Trinitarian formula is spoken. The root meaning of the word *baptize* is to "plunge or to immerse," and the ritual text gives prominence to the ancient custom of Baptism by immersion. (For more about Baptism by immersion, see the Appendix.) The **explanatory rites** of clothing with a baptismal garment (an optional rite) and presenting a lighted candle follow.

Confirmation begins with an invitation to pray, proceeds with the **laying on of hands** and the prayer invoking the Holy Spirit, continues through the **anointing with chrism,** and concludes with the sign of peace extended by the minister of the sacrament. The restoration of the close connection between Baptism and Confirmation is one of the great achievements of the ritual of the Church today. So important is this connection that Confirmation may not be deferred to another time (unless a truly extraordinary situation exists), and priests who baptize are given the faculty to confirm by the very law of the Church, so that the two sacraments will remain together in the same celebration. The rite itself articulates the most powerful of theological reasons for always keeping Baptism and Confirmation together:

> The conjunction of the two celebrations signifies the unity of the paschal mystery, the close link between the mission of the Son and the outpouring of the Holy Spirit, and the connection between the two sacraments through which the Son and the Holy Spirit come with the Father to those who are baptized. (RCIA 215)

After the renewal of baptismal promises by the assembly and a sprinkling with baptismal water, the liturgy continues with the **general intercessions,** in which the neophytes participate for the first time, and the **presentation of the gifts** of bread and wine, which are brought forward by the neophytes (RCIA 241). The **Eucharist,** which is "the climax of their initiation and the center of the whole Christian life" (RCIA 243), then takes place. The festive grandeur of this portion of the liturgy is unmistakable, as Christ, our paschal sacrifice, is shared. The risen Christ presides over the meal and is himself our food and drink for eternal life. The Eucharist foreshadows the eschatological banquet at the end of time, the banquet of heaven, a feast of Reconciliation and joy that never ends. For the first time, the neophytes share in eucharistic communion—the consummate act of membership in the Church, the Body of Christ. There are no special rubrics for the neophytes' reception of communion, except for the direction that the celebrant may highlight this important moment before the general invitation to communion ("This is the Lamb of God . . ." see RCIA 243), and for the instruction that they and their godparents, parents, spouses and catechists receive communion under both forms (RCIA 243). Certainly at such a festive occasion it would be desirable for the whole assembly to receive communion under both forms.

Finally, the dismissal, which ends the Easter Vigil triumphantly, sends us forth from the entire triduum to live the good news of the resurrection. Neither the Mass of the Lord's Supper on Holy Thursday, nor the Celebration of the Lord's Passion on Good Friday end with a dismissal because the triduum is one great liturgy celebrated over the course of three days. The Easter Vigil is the culmination and highlight of the triduum, and from this crowning liturgy of the triduum we are at last sent forth. It is important therefore that the dismissal at the end of the Easter Vigil be strong and jubilant.

Discernment Before the Sacraments of Initiation

Discernment for the celebration of the sacraments of initiation is completed before the "Rite of Election/Call to Continuing Conversion." No formal discernment is needed beyond this. However participants are always encouraged to pay attention to how they feel God is inviting them to grow, change, let go, or come closer to God. Much of this discernment will happen through the scrutiny celebrations.

Spiritual Preparation of the Elect and Candidates

The primary preparation is liturgical. The "Scrutinies" and "Penitential Rite" deepen the knowledge and understanding of letting go of sin and being drawn into God's grace through an intimate relationship with Christ, who is the Living Water, the Light of the World, and the Resurrection and the Life. Both the elect's and candidate's reflection on their experience and further prayer deepen this awareness. Those preparing for reception into the full communion of the Catholic Church are encouraged to celebrate the sacrament of Reconciliation as a way of renewing their baptismal life. Participating in the entire Easter triduum and the "Preparation Rites" on Holy Saturday (see page 90) is the immediate preparation for the celebration of the sacraments of initiation. Some parishes provide a day or overnight retreat to assist those being initiated in prayerful preparation. (See *Purification and Enlightenment Resource Book,* pages 123–135, in the *Foundations in Faith* series.)

Preparing the Ministers

The ministers for the sacraments at the Easter Vigil will need their usual preparation for the celebration of the Easter Vigil. In addition the godparents, sponsors, parents of children who will be initiated, the presider, director of initiation, and cantor will need to rehearse, primarily to know their general placement and way of participating in the rite. This rehearsal may occur before or after the "Preparation Rites" or time of prayer with the elect and the baptized candidates.

Engaging the Assembly

The long range preparation of the assembly for the celebration of the sacraments of initiation occurs in various ways including:
- ✦ Participating in the "Rite of Acceptance" and the "Rite of Sending."
- ✦ Participating in the scrutinies.
- ✦ Focusing on the parish's lenten journey as a time of renewal of Baptism.
- ✦ Praying at parish gatherings for those being initiated.

More immediate preparation includes:
- ✦ Participating in the entire triduum.
- ✦ Making a deliberate attempt to set aside the three days of the triduum as a time of prayer, perhaps using a resource, such as *What Am I Doing for the Triduum This Year?* (Paul Turner, LTP), individually or in groups.
- ✦ Fasting on Holy Saturday in anticipation of the Easter Vigil.
- ✦ Participating in liturgical preparations for the Vigil (music, environment, and so on) and in preparations for a reception following it.

Environment

Preparing the environment for the Easter Vigil normally involves working with several sites where the liturgical action takes place. The place of the fire, the setting where the Word is proclaimed, the place of Baptism, and the altar area all deserve attention.

A large fire is needed for a large assembly. Its setting should be spartan, and once the people have gathered there, all outdoor lights should be shut off. Many people have to move around the fire area in semidarkness without tripping—that the area should be uncluttered goes without saying. The same is true of the assembly area inside the church where the people will process with lighted candles and stand in semidarkness for the Exsultet.

Some lights should be put on for the Liturgy of the Word. The light can grow as the Vigil progresses, but too sharp a contrast in lighting between the Old and the New Testament readings creates an unfortunate suggestion of the inferiority of the Old, which is not the point. Besides people have to read music and texts. With a medium range of lighting, candles placed near the ambo and in the assembly area, a sense of keeping vigil in the night can still maintain. Full lighting is indicated from the Gloria onward.

Many churches have built permanent immersion fonts in recent years, but churches that do not have a permanent font can construct a temporary one (see Appendix). A variety of designs are pictured in Regina Kuehn's *A Place for Baptism* (LTP). A garden atmosphere around the font may be lovely but impractical; beware of floral arrangements that get in the way of liturgical actions. A place to enshrine the sacred chrism also may be constructed near the font. When using any temporary space, check to see if the existing lighting is adequate for the spot you choose. If not, experiment with supplemental lighting.

The outdoor sound system that you used for the "Rite of Acceptance" (see p. 24) should stand you in good stead for the Vigil—with only one mike for the presider. Inside the church, besides providing amplification for the usual ministers, see that some microphones are available for the elect and the candidates who each speak a profession of faith.

Eucharist is what we do in our churches all the time, so we are well set up for this portion of the liturgy. Take a fresh look at your altar area for the Vigil, however. How does it speak the paschal mystery during this holy night? How does it compare with the other liturgical spaces that you have created for the preceding portions of the liturgy?

Music

The Easter Vigil is a most festive occasion. If possible, the eucharistic prayer and the gospel reading should be sung. Individual cantors, choir, and special instruments such as bells, brass and percussion can do much to enhance the music of this night; yet the liturgical musician's greatest instrument is a singing congregation, and everything must be done to help this instrument attain its full potential.

Musical resources for the Easter Vigil abound from time-honored chants to brand new compositions. Although this liturgy takes place but once a year, like all of the liturgies of the triduum it has its musical traditions within each community, and these traditions should be respected. Psalmody is particularly important to the Vigil. Although the readings can be followed by periods of silence, the beauty of the psalms are a significant aspect of the glory of this night.

With regard to specific music for the initiatory parts of the liturgy, there is much overlap between the rites that are celebrated at the Easter Vigil and the initiation sacraments celebrated at other times of the year. Acclamations such as "Springs of water, bless the Lord" and "You have put on Christ," if placed on the assembly's lips frequently during the year, will become well known. A consistent musical repertoire for such acclamations can help the assembly to own them.

The Vigil includes many beautiful, lengthy prayer texts. The blessing of the fire, the Exsultet, the blessing of the water, the prayer of Confirmation are examples. Some of these may be effectively sung by one voice, a capella. Others may benefit from having an instrument or a choir enhance them, or having them interspersed with sung acclamations by the assembly. The question is: how will the assembly be helped by the musical choices to enter into the spirit of this prayer?

In choosing repertoire, it is important not only to evaluate musical quality and appropriateness but also to evaluate textual choices carefully, checking them against the material in the ritual book. Has a composer, perhaps unwittingly, changed the meaning of a prayer by altering its text? Are there better choices available?

Homily Suggestions

The very first resource to prepare for preaching at the Easter Vigil is the Lectionary and its series of Scripture readings and psalm texts from the Old Testament that summarize for the believing community the salvation history that leads us up to Christ. This is followed by the sublime epistle selection from Paul's Letter to the Romans. The gospel pericope changes with each year of the three-year cycle.

Homilists will want to reflect upon these texts and the appropriate commentaries. In addition, however, homilists will also be served by studying the prayer texts found in the Sacramentary and the *Rite of Christian Initiation of Adults*. Their study could also be rounded out by checking the texts of the readings and prayers found in the Liturgy of the Hours.

In perusing all this material, to what do we pay particular attention? Preachers must use the words, phrases, and images that leap off the page and into the heart proclaiming the ancient and once-again newness of the drama of salvation found in Christ. *Sin has been vanquished. Death is put to death. O death, you are done for, you are finished! Christ is risen and we are clothed in the garments of light, new life, an eternal hope, heralded for all ages and all peoples!*

The homily can contain a narrative, a story. It can be fashioned like a litany, with one phrase rolling after the other, reaching a thunderous conclusion. It can be structured in many different ways. But if the homily lacks coherence, if it wanders, if it does not succinctly and powerfully reflect the dazzling blinding brilliance of God's good news in the resurrection of Christ—then what is the point of preaching?

Preparing to preach and then actually delivering a thoughtful, rousing, or provoking homily on this night is a daunting task. And yet it can be done. The homilist might ask: What does this celebration mean to me? The crux is resurrection. How has the resurrection changed *my* life?

It is the job of the homilist to be excited and to convey that excitement to those assembled. Tonight, people want to be excited. They want to be reminded; they want to vigil through this deep, dark night into the light of Christ. They want to drown in the waters of new life and rise with the Lord as his Spirit quickens hearts of faith. They want to be filled, nourished, and sated by the meal that only Christ can provide, that only those gathered around the table of the Lord can find. They want to be so fired up that they cannot wait to go forth and proclaim by their words and deeds that Christ is risen—he is truly risen.

Decisions That Need To Be Made

How Will the Assembly Be Active and Involved?

Here are some ideas:

✧ The way the assembly gathers on this night is unusual (in darkness, out of doors) and important. Advance communication and a good ministry of hospitality are necessary to assure safety and comfort and to allow people to attend to what is happening without undue distraction. It is necessary to provide realistic options for participation of the disabled and those who find it difficult to stand for long periods.

✧ Musical responses and acclamations occur throughout the Vigil. Music that is well-known and can be sung without printed materials is highly desirable, especially in this liturgy, which involves much action, many processions, and which takes place partially in the dark. Creative use of acclamations for the Exsultet, the blessing of water and the prayer of Confirmation can help to engage the assembly in these beautiful, but long, prayer texts.

✧ Movement refreshes the assembly and should be included wherever possible. For example, rather than sprinkle the assembly after the renewal of Baptism, they could come to the font to receive the blessed water. We have already mentioned a movement of the assembly from outside to inside during the Service of Light.

✧ Include in the Litany of the Saints the patron saints of those being initiated and other saints important to the local community.

How Will We Highlight the Central Symbols?

Here are some ideas:

✧ Begin the liturgy not only after sunset but after the darkness has settled. Court the darkness. In urban areas explore the possibility of turning out street lights near the place where the fire will be lit.

✧ Construct a large fire out of doors for the assembly to gather around. The primal symbol of light piercing the darkness speaks of creation and new life.

✧ Proclaim all seven Old Testament readings, using a variety of voices, styles and musical responses. If your community is not used to proclaiming all the readings, work up to this gradually, adding an additional reading each year.

- Use plenty of water for Baptism (see Appendix). Construct a numinous, substantial font that speaks of both death and resurrection. There should be enough water "to die in." Make it look dangerous.

- Use plenty of oil for Confirmation. The assembly should be able to identify a neophyte with their eyes closed—by the scent of chrism, an Easter smell.

- Use fresh baked bread and plenty of wine for the Eucharist. Do not skimp on these central symbols. Let the Eucharist be the grand feast for which we have fasted—a foretaste of the banquet of heaven.

- The candidates for Baptism are a symbol of the paschal mystery. Make sure that their voices can be heard by all. Make sure that they can be seen by all, and that any baptismal garments they wear and candles they hold are beautiful things, full-sized, simple, and dignified.

- The godparents symbolize the care of the whole community for the neophytes. They should be unobtrusive yet identifiable and visible during the rite—placing a hand on the shoulder of their godchild, guiding and helping as needed. Catechists too should have an active role presenting the candidates to the assembly and assisting in the ritual. For example, the catechist could bring forward and pour out the sacred chrism for Confirmation.

Tips for Presiders

Here are some general considerations:

- As much as possible, *relax* during Holy Saturday. Pray and reflect in a quiet place. Naturally, the liturgy committee and the initiation team may want you to be in church all day helping to set up, perhaps assisting with the server and the godparent practices. Clear your calendar, eliminating all but the most essential events so that you can mentally, physically, and spiritually prepare for this night's liturgy. The Easter Vigil is very demanding for the presider and other ministers. Take care of yourself during the day so that you can give this Vigil what it deserves.

- This is not a liturgy that we do often. Take the time to *study* and *review* it. With all the liturgical preparations for the Vigil finished well ahead of the end of Lent, including a unified sequence set down on paper, you should be able to spend the days immediately before the Easter triduum reviewing the four major components of the Vigil and their details. Especially if you will be presiding over various types of initiation within the same liturgy (Baptism, reception, and completion of Christian initiation), you will want to review and commit to memory the sequence of these rites.

- Throughout the celebration of this liturgy, *pace* yourself. As presiding celebrant, you will help guide the assembly and the elect through the various movements of this Vigil. It is a long, beautiful, and elaborate liturgy that in all of its detail and abundance is highly charged and evocative. Guiding everyone else through the celebration of the Vigil will take lots of energy and require pacing on your part, in order to put maximum energy where it is required: during the profession of faith and Baptism(s), during the receptions (if they are done on this night), during the anointing with chrism, and during the eucharistic prayer.

- *Learn the names* of the elect before the Vigil celebration. Nothing could be worse than a presider who is initiating to be searching for name tags in order to identify those in the community who are being plunged into the waters of rebirth or who are completing their initiation!

Here are some specific considerations:

- Because this liturgy begins after sundown and with all the lights turned out (we hope that weather permitting you are outside with the outdoor lights also turned off), you will need a very small penlight in order to find your way around. If your eyes are good enough, consider using only the *light of the fire* in order to see the presidential prayers at the beginning for the blessing of the fire and the preparation of the Easter candle. To do so, however, the presider notebook or the Sacramentary must be positioned so that the new fire casts light upon the pages.

- If you are baptizing by immersion, and if the pool is big enough, consider entering the water before the elect—both to help them in and as an act of hospitality by joining them in the baptismal font. Since you are probably going to be wearing the best chasuble of the parish for the Vigil, you may want to remove it (and your shoes and socks) before getting into the font. Make provisions for a change of dry clothes, including alb and stole, after the Baptism(s).

- Set aside your own squeamishness. Boldly pour lots of water over those you are baptizing. A few drips and dabs will not signal to them or to the assembly that they are dying with Christ. They will want—and as presider you will supply them with—a semblance of what it is like to be drowning.

- While the rite is clear that for Confirmation the right thumb of the celebrant is dipped into the chrism, this does not exclude the use of your entire right hand and palm in order to anoint. The characteristic of this liturgy is lavish abundance, and the way in which the anointings are done should signal this lavishness of God's grace to the elect and the assembly of the faithful.

◆ You may not be the most accomplished of singers, but consider singing or chanting the eucharistic prayer. Chant will be easier than singing. Simple chant patterns are provided in the Sacramentary. The Rite emphasizes that the Eucharist is the high point of initiation, its culmination. Singing or chanting the eucharistic prayer—given the utter elaborateness of what has already occurred—may give it greater weight for balance in the overall liturgy of this night.

◆ Check the rubric at RCIA 243 concerning the Eucharist as the center of our life. Without making this little instruction another homily, you may want to carefully craft a beautiful reminder to the neophytes as they prepare to come forward and receive the Lord.

Baptized Candidates: What's Different?

The combined rite for the Easter Vigil (RCIA 562–594) places the renewal of baptismal promises *before* Confirmation (when the combined rite is not used [see RCIA 236], the assembly's renewal of baptismal promises comes last). The Rite furthermore incorporates the "Rite of Reception into the Full Communion of the Catholic Church" into the liturgy after the assembly renews its baptismal promises. The renewal of baptismal commitment, therefore, serves as the profession of faith for those to be received into full communion, as well as for the rest of the assembly.

The newly-baptized and the newly-received then celebrate Confirmation together. The order of this combined rite facilitates the smooth flow of the liturgy when Baptism is celebrated by immersion, as the newly-baptized have time to change into dry clothing while the renewal of baptismal promises and the "Rite of Reception" is taking place.

If there is no "Rite of Reception" at the Easter Vigil, Confirmation may take place either at the font or in the sanctuary. But when the "Rite of Reception" is included, Confirmation takes place in the sanctuary.

An unfortunate weakness of the combined rite is that it completely overlooks the place of the baptized but uncatechized adult Catholic candidates, who also normally find the high point of their formation in the Easter Vigil, where they celebrate Confirmation and Eucharist (RCIA 409). A necessary adaption for those communities that include baptized Catholic candidates is to call them forward by name after the "Rite of Reception" and acknowledge their particular identity in some way at that time. All three groups are then confirmed together.

Two minor points about the baptized candidates also deserve notice. The presentation of a baptismal garment is an optional rite for adults. If the newly-baptized are, however, to be presented with baptismal garments, it would be fitting for the baptized candidates to be clad in such garments from the beginning of the celebration. The baptized candidates also fully participate in the Service of Light carrying lighted candles with the rest of the assembly. The elect do not carry a lighted candle until they receive one at their Baptism.

What About Children?

Children of catechetical age take part in all the sacraments of initiation at the Easter Vigil in the same way that adults do. It is especially important to remember that the Confirmation of these children is not deferred to a later occasion but must be celebrated at the time they are baptized (RCIA 305; RCIA, NS 18).

D. After the Rite

Evaluation of the Celebration of the Easter Sacraments

Take some time within ten days after the celebration of the Easter sacraments at the Easter Vigil to evaluate what went well, what did not, and what needs to be changed for next year's celebration. Some people who you may wish to involve in the evaluation are: the coordinator, the presider, the liturgist, the music director, and some additional team members. In addition to a core group of those who will reflect on the experience of this liturgy, input may be elicited from others in the parish.

A process similar to this one may be helpful:

1. Evaluators reflect on their experience, using the format on page 66, which may be duplicated as needed.
2. Each evaluator elicits responses from three parishioners who participated in this liturgy.
3. The evaluators come together to talk about their experience and make appropriate suggestions for the next celebration of this (and possibly other) major rites.
4. The coordinator meets with appropriate persons to talk about these changes.

Evaluation: Easter Vigil Celebration of the Sacraments of Initiation

The rites celebrated were: _____ Baptism, Confirmation, and Eucharist for the Elect

_____ Reception, Confirmation, and Eucharist for Non-Catholic Baptized Candidates

_____ Confirmation and Eucharist for Catholic Candidates

Date of celebration _____ Time of celebration _____

Number of adults and children of catechetical age who were baptized _____

Number who were received into full communion _____

Number of Catholics completing their initiation _____

1. For me the highlight of the celebration was _____

    because _____ .

2. For me the part of the celebration that was least meaningful was _____

    because _____ .

3. If I were to describe the important parts of this celebration to others, I would tell them _____

    _____ .

4. Rate the following on a scale of 1–10 (1 is low, 10 is high) on how well
    this part of the rite was celebrated and give a reason for your response.

    _____ The lighting of the Easter fire _____

    _____ The procession into the church _____

    _____ The proclamation of the Exsultet _____

    _____ The Liturgy of the Word _____

    _____ The Litany of the Saints _____

    _____ The blessing of the baptismal water _____

    _____ The Baptisms _____

    _____ The receptions into full communion _____

    _____ The celebration of Confirmation _____

    _____ The celebration of the Eucharist _____

    _____ The music that supported the liturgical action of the rite _____

    _____ The music that was sung well by the assembly _____

5. If I were to change something in how this rite is celebrated next year, I would suggest _____

    _____

    because _____ .

6. Other details that need to be remembered for the next celebration of the Easter Vigil are: _____

    _____ .

Mystagogy

Gather the neophytes and various members of the community within a few days of the Easter Vigil. Specifically invite the choir, the musicians, the lectors, and the eucharistic ministers who were present at the Easter Vigil, men and women initiated in previous years, past sponsors and godparents, as well as the general assembly. The invitation for this reflection on the Easter Vigil should be included in the parish bulletin when the times of the triduum celebrations are published.

Besides this reflection session, several additional options may be found on pages 47–49 of *Mystagogia Resource Book* in the *Foundations in Faith* series.

Reflecting on the Easter Vigil with the Neophytes

Gathering

1. Gather in the worship space around the font with the Easter candle lighted, a vessel of chrism, bread and wine, and spring flowers, or in another suitable space with the environment prepared with these Easter symbols. Have the neophytes wear their white baptismal robes.

2. Welcome everyone. Invite the various groupings of those gathered to stand as you name them: newly baptized, those received into the full communion of the Catholic Church, Catholic candidates who completed their initiation, godparents and sponsors, family members of those initiated, ministers at the Easter Vigil, and members of the assembly. Give this introduction: *Tonight we gather in a special way with those who received the sacraments of initiation only a few nights ago. We ask them to share with us what they experienced in Baptism, Confirmation, and Eucharist. We all share how God spoke to us at the Easter Vigil celebration. Let us join together this night in the spirit of the Risen Christ.* Next say: *Alleluia, He is risen!* Ask everyone to repeat this acclamation as you say it again. Then sing together "God Is Alive" (Haas, GIA Publications) or another Easter hymn.

3. Pray this prayer:
Loving and gracious God, Christ is risen. Christ is truly risen, and we with him. You have formed us anew in Christ. You have brought us through the waters of Baptism to new life with you. You are holy and wonderful, and we are grateful! Make us aware of all you have done and are doing in us. Open our eyes and hearts to understand more fully our Baptism, Confirmation, and oneness at the table of the Lord's Body and Blood. Inspire us this evening with the Spirit who hovers around us and breathes within us. We ask this through Christ, the Risen One. Amen.

Remembering

1. Invite everyone to reflect on their experience, saying:
Let's take a few moments to go inside ourselves and breathe. God's own Spirit breathes within us. Go back in time to when you first arrived before the Easter Vigil—where you gathered, what you were thinking and feeling. Recall the various sounds, smells, lighting, people, and memories of God speaking to you that night. (Pause.) *We gathered and the new fire was lighted in the darkness. We brought the light of Christ into the church and sang the glorious hymn, the Exultet. We listened to the stories of our salvation from creation, to the Israelites crossing the Red Sea, to God's gracious love and mercy. We sang the Gloria and the church was lighted! The sights of new life greeted us. We heard the proclamation that Christ has been raised. After the homily* (include some images from the homily if you wish) *the Litany of the Saints was sung and we processed to the baptismal font and blessed the water. Those to be baptized were called forth, professed their faith, and were baptized. Others were received into full communion with the Catholic Church. Our Catholic candidates were called forward to join them. All were sealed with the fragrant chrism in Confirmation. We gathered as*

one baptized community around the Table of the Lord for the eucharistic prayer. Some among us ate and drank the Body and Blood of the Lord for the first time. This entire community, this living body of Christ, was sent forth to live our Easter faith.

2. Invite people to keep their eyes still closed and to call out a word or phrase naming a part of this celebration that was powerful for them. Allow several minutes for these responses. When they are finished, ask people to open their eyes and return to this space.

3. Name the various groups.

   A. Those who were baptized.

   B. Those who were received into the Catholic Church.

   C. Those Catholics who completed their initiation at the Vigil.

   D. Godparents, sponsors, and parents of children who were initiated.

   E. Ministers or members of the assembly.

   Ask volunteers from each group to stand and share something of their experience at the Vigil. For example, ask those who were baptized to speak of what they experienced in their Baptism, Confirmation, or Eucharist.

4. Ask everyone to reflect on these questions and share their responses in groups of three with the persons sitting around them. Hand these questions out on paper.

   From the Easter Vigil,

   A. What experience of God do you want to take with you?

   B. What does Baptism now mean to you?

   C. How would you describe who we are as Church, and how we are to live in the world?

5. After about ten minutes, invite some responses in the large group to the questions one at a time.

Prayer

Invite everyone to stand around the baptismal font and Easter candle. Have a lector proclaim Romans 6:3–11. Sing together a joyful Alleluia. Give this invitation: *As the living Body of Christ, let us offer one another the peace of Christ, and exchange the sign of peace with one another.*

Rite of Reception
Outside the Easter Vigil

A. Overview of the Rite

The Rite at a Glance

LITURGY OF THE WORD

    Readings

    Homily

CELEBRATION OF RECEPTION

    Invitation

    Profession of Faith

    Act of Reception

    [Confirmation]

        Laying on of hands

        Anointing with Chrism

    Celebrant's Sign of Welcome

    General Intercessions

    Sign of Peace

LITURGY OF THE EUCHARIST

Understanding the Rite

Those baptized candidates who are uncatechized undertake a process of formation very similar to that to the catechumens. They pass through the same stages and periods of the initiation process as do the unbaptized, and although the rituals are adapted to reflect their baptized status, the culmination of their initiation in the sacraments of Confirmation and Eucharist normally takes place with the elect at the Easter Vigil (RCIA 409), using the combined rite (RCIA 562 ff.).

For those baptized candidates from other Christian denominations who are catechized, however, a process as all-inclusive as the catechumen's is unnecessary. An individual determination of the needs of such candidates must be made. As the "National Statutes for the Catechumenate" of the U.S. edition makes clear: "Those baptized persons who have lived as Christians and need only instruction in the Catholic tradition and a degree of probation within the Catholic community should not be asked to undergo a full program parallel to the catechumenate" (RCIA, NS 31).

Given the fact that the preparation time of catechized candidates will be shorter and its culmination will not be at the Easter Vigil, the completion of the process of reception into full communion takes place in the midst of the community of the faithful at Sunday Mass at what is called the "Rite of Reception."

Several elements taken together make up the "Rite of Reception." The celebration begins with the **Liturgy of the Word,** which may use readings from the Sunday Lectionary, or from the "Rite of Reception" itself (RCIA 501) or from the Mass for the Unity of Christians. The Liturgy of the Word is followed by both a profession of faith, that is, a **creed** spoken along with the assembly, and a **profession of Catholic faith**—a short, pithy statement affirming in principle all the essentials of Catholic belief. This statement is meant to contain no more than what is strictly necessary, and should not be adapted or expanded in any way. It may be spoken as a statement or answered as a question. There is no abjuration of heresy in the rite. Following the profession of faith, the **Act of Reception** welcomes the person into the community of faith.

Then if the candidate has not already been validly confirmed, the sacrament of **Confirmation** is celebrated. A priest who receives candidates into full communion who are not validly confirmed must confirm them at the same celebration (canons 883:2 and 885:2). They cannot receive the Eucharist until they have been confirmed (RCIA, NS 35). A special **gesture of welcome** from the celebrant of the rite follows Confirmation; and after **intercessions** are prayed, the whole assembly joins in a **sign of peace** which extends the embrace of the whole community to the newly-received. The sign of peace is omitted later in the liturgy.

The **Eucharist** then follows. Eucharistic communion is undoubtedly the high point of the "Rite of Reception" for which the other elements prepare (RCIA 475.1). Unity at the Table of the Lord is the goal of the "Rite of Reception." In that unity the newly-received Catholic joins the whole Catholic Church in its prayer for all people and especially for the ongoing journey toward unity of all Christian churches and communities. Again if the rite takes place on a solemnity or a Sunday, the Mass of the day is used but at other occasions the Mass for the Unity of Christians is used.

B. Preparing the Community

Discernment Before the Rite of Reception

Discerning Whether the Candidates Are Catechized

Baptized candidates with little or no catechesis participate in a process similar to the catechumens. Discernment about their initiation occurs in a similar way to that of catechumens. (See the sections in this guide on discernment before each of the major rites.) Many baptized candidates, however, come with a more developed experience of catechesis and faith formation. Rather than participating in a catechumenate-like structure, their formation is determined according to their individual needs. The initial discernment is to identify which of these two courses to follow.

Discerning What Is Needed for the Catechized

Baptized candidates with catechetical formation are not all alike. Initially, no specific date is set for celebrating the "Rite of Reception." The candidates need to be aware that some formation is usually desirable and the amount of time cannot be determined at the outset. Individual discernment with each person is needed and will include the following:

✦ What is drawing the person to live their baptismal journey within the Catholic tradition? Why are they doing this now?

✦ What are their concerns about living their faith within the Catholic tradition?

✦ How supportive is their family and how does this affect them?

✦ What is their Christian faith background, formation, and practice?

✦ In what ways is God inviting them to change in their life?

Catechetical Formation

The four foundational areas of word, worship, community, and mission (see RCIA 75) give a basis for determining the degree to which a person is catechized and what further formation is needed. Each of these four areas are explored with the candidates through individual conversation, in small faith-sharing groups, and/or in gatherings with some team members and others in the community.

Word

✦ Moving from literal knowledge about the Scriptures to responding to their meaning in personal ways in daily life.

- ✧ Having a relationship with Christ as well as knowing about his life and teachings.
- ✧ Having a basic understanding of the Catholic Church, its teachings and its traditions.
- ✧ Accepting the Church as the authoritative interpreter of Scripture, and Tradition as the privileged place of divine Revelation.
- ✧ Appreciating God's presence and nourishment in the Word.
- ✧ Knowing the Word is the living Word of God.

Worship

- ✧ Valuing worship with the community.
- ✧ Allowing worship to challenge and nurture them.
- ✧ Understanding the sacramental nature of the Catholic Church.
- ✧ Bringing their life of prayer and action to worship, and having worship inform their life of prayer and action.
- ✧ Appreciating that the Church, the living Body of Christ, prays through, with, and in Christ.

Community

- ✧ Seeing themselves as part of the Church's communal life.
- ✧ Participating in appropriate activities of the Church, including social, charity and justice, formation, service, and prayer opportunities.
- ✧ Seeing their life as a disciple integrally connected to the life, death, and resurrection of Christ and the living body of Christ, the Church.
- ✧ Knowing their life is not independent but interdependent.

Mission

- ✧ Knowing the Church participates in Christ's mission of bringing about God's reign in the world in real ways.
- ✧ Being willing to give and receive, to serve and be served, as is appropriate to further God's work in the world.
- ✧ Realizing their particular call to service and witness.
- ✧ Understanding the Church's call—and theirs—to promote the dignity and rights of all people in neighborhoods, in the Church, and in the world.
- ✧ Responding to the gospel call to live justly.

No one is perfect in fulfilling all of these dimensions of catechetical formation. However, the candidates need to give attention to these four essential aspects of living the Catholic faith

in their formation process—whether exploring these areas in individual discussions or small group sharing, or participating in various Church activities, or reflecting on them. When the person seems to have an understanding and appreciation of this Catholic way of life, an individual discernment interview is scheduled.

Discernment Interview Before Setting a Date for the Rite of Reception

Explore with the candidate what effect this formation has had on his or her life. Invite some sharing around some of the following areas:

- ✧ What new insights do they have about the Catholic Church?
- ✧ What has surprised and delighted them about the Church?
- ✧ What do they find difficult about the Church?
- ✧ How has their relationship with God been affected during this formation time?
- ✧ How have their relationships with others (spouse, children, coworkers) been affected?
- ✧ In what ways have they changed?
- ✧ In what ways do they sense God is inviting them to further growth?
- ✧ What concerns or questions do they have about the Catholic Church?
- ✧ Are they ready to make a lifetime commitment to the Catholic Church?

Setting a Date for the Rite of Reception

When the candidate shows signs of readiness, look for a date on the parish calendar when the "Rite of Reception" is able to be celebrated well. Allow time for immediate spiritual preparation before this rite is celebrated.

- ✧ Choose a time at a Sunday Mass or when a portion of the community is able to be present.
- ✧ Avoid major liturgical feasts and seasons when the focus of the liturgy is elsewhere (e.g., Advent and Lent).

Immediate Spiritual Preparation of the Candidates for Celebrating the Rite of Reception

Each candidate will have a sponsor to accompany him or her while preparing for the "Rite of Reception." This sponsor, family members, and the parish faith communities that have been assisting with the candidate's preparation will be part of this time of prayer that precedes the celebration of the rite. As the date for the "Rite of Reception" nears, several options for spiritual preparation present themselves.

  ✧ A day, evening, or overnight retreat, preferably away from the parish grounds. (See *Purification and Enlightenment Resource Book,* pages 123–135, in the *Foundations in Faith* series for suggestions.)

  ✧ A penitential service with encouragement to celebrate the sacrament of Penance.

  ✧ A time of faith-sharing with the sponsor or within a parish faith community.

  ✧ A celebration of the Liturgy of the Hours.

Penitential Service

During the course of their catechetical formation, the candidates should be given an introduction to the sacrament of Penance and its place in the life of the Church. Myths, questions, and misunderstandings may need to be addressed before the candidates will feel comfortable in celebrating the sacrament themselves for the first time. (Note: Non-Catholic candidates are able to celebrate this sacrament before the "Rite of Reception." See RCIA, NS 36.)

There are three forms of the sacrament of Penance:

  ✧ Reconciliation of individual penitents.

  ✧ Communal Reconciliation with individual confessions and absolution.

  ✧ General absolution (not practiced except in extraordinary circumstances).

The choice of whether to celebrate the sacrament according to form one or form two is an important one for the first experience of sacramental Reconciliation.

Some may wish to take advantage of the first form, so that they will have more time for their individual confession and for receiving counsel from the priest. No one should feel rushed; it is important that the pastoral care of the Church be experienced in the celebration of this sacrament of healing. On the other hand, participation in a communal celebration of Reconciliation is a wonderful reminder that others are seeking forgiveness as well, and that the sacrament of Penance not only makes peace between ourselves and God but also restores communion with the Church and strengthens the bonds of charity and love that make us one people. The sacrament of Penance is at its heart a renewal of Baptism. The Christian turns away from what holds back from following Christ, and renews the commitment to follow Christ.

In addition to the catechetical preparation, spiritual preparation for the sacrament of Penance may be furthered by the celebration of penitential services apart from the sacrament. The *Rite of Christian Initiation of Adults* encourages these for uncatechized candidates (RCIA 408), and several models can be found in Appendix II of the *Rite of Penance.* Here is one example of such a penitential service. It follows the basic form of the "Penitential Service" given in the *Rite of Penance.* The form may be adapted when the sacrament of Penance is not celebrated. The prayers, actions, and hymns focus on baptismal renewal. Encourage the sponsor and/or family members to accompany the candidate to celebrate the sacrament with the priest the candidate chooses sometime after this prayer and before the "Rite of Reception."

Sample Penitential Service

Introductory Rites

Hymn:
  "We Are Called" (Haas, GIA Publications) or another
  appropriate hymn.

Greeting

Introduction

Prayer

Celebration of the Word of God

First Reading:
> Ephesians 3:14–21, 1 Corinthians 12:31–13:13,
> Colossians 3:12–17, or Ephesians 5: 8–14

Responsorial Psalm

Gospel:
> Matthew 5:1–12, Matthew 5:13–16, Matthew 6:19–33,
> or John 13:1–17

Homily

Liturgy of Repentance

Examination of Conscience
> Use concerns that relate to the candidate's life. Include
> such areas as:
> - Prayer, use of time, material possessions, place of
>   God in life,
> - Family/relationship struggles, service, and justice
>   outreach.

Prayer of Sorrow:
> Allow some silent reflection time. If the number of
> those gathered is small, individuals may pray aloud.

Laying on of Hands:
> Use this or some other ritual action involving the
> Church's primary symbols. For example, all may light a
> candle from the Easter candle, to signify that all the
> baptized are enlightened by Christ.

Lord's Prayer

Concluding Rites

Prayer

Sign of Peace

Dismissal

Hymn:
> "For the Life of the World" (Haas, GIA Publications)

Liturgy of the Hours

Have the candidates with their sponsors participate in a parish
celebration of Morning Prayer or Evening Prayer from the
Liturgy of the Hours. Explain the importance of praying the
Psalms and marking time as sacred. You may also wish to
explain how the rosary developed out of the Liturgy of the
Hours.

Sharing and Prayer as Spiritual Preparation for the Rite of Reception

Gathering

1. Gather near the font. Welcome the candidates, sponsors, family members, and other members of the parish.
2. Ask participants to focus on the font. Pray a prayer in your own words asking God to deepen and bring into fullness the Baptism of these candidates and all who are assembled.

Reflection

1. Have a team member proclaim Matthew 17:1–8.

2. Invite everyone to listen as the reading is proclaimed again and name a word or phrase that speaks in a special way to them. Proclaim Matthew 17:1–8. Invite participants to say the word or phrase aloud.

3. State the following: *This description of Jesus' transfiguration provides us with an image of who we are as the baptized. We are filled with light. We, too, are God's beloved son or daughter. God's favor rests on us.* Then invite reflection, saying: *After this time of preparation for full communion, or being involved in this preparation, in what new ways are you aware that you are God's beloved? How does this affect you in your day-to-day life?* Have the participants share their responses in sponsor/candidate and other pairs. Then invite some sharing in the total group.

4. Ask participants to reflect on these questions and share responses in their sponsor/candidate and other pairs: *What old patterns, thoughts, behaviors have you left behind? What new awareness and beliefs do you carry with you?* Allow about 15 minutes. Then invite participants to share some of their experiences in the total group.

5. Make these points:
   - Over and over again we come to understand what it means that we are God's beloved.
   - All we have and are is a result of God's grace and gift, not what we do.
   - Living as baptized followers of Christ calls us to continual change and conversion.
   - As the baptized, we walk with Christ in light moment-by-moment.
   - As Church, we encourage, support, and challenge one another in our Christian faith, and to live the mission of Jesus.

6. Ask the participants to reflect on these questions: *How does the Catholic Church provide support for you in living your Christian faith? In what ways does the Catholic Church challenge you to live your Christian faith more deeply?* Invite the participants to share their responses in their pairs. When they are ready, elicit some responses in the total group.

Prayer

1. Have a lector or parish member proclaim Colossians 3:12–17.
2. Invite anyone to pray in his or her own words, using this invitation: *Let's take a few minutes of quiet, and pray for (name) as he or she prepares for reception into the full communion of the Catholic Church. Let's also pray for ourselves and for our Church. (Pause for two or three minutes.) I invite anyone who wishes to express a prayer aloud at this time to do so.*
3. Invite the candidates and sponsors, and others to come in pairs to the baptismal font. Ask them to take some water and bless the candidate or other person on the forehead, heart, and hands with the holy water.
4. Sing "How Shall I Sing to God?" (Haas, GIA Publications) or another familiar hymn.

Preparing the Ministers

The celebration of the "Rite of Reception" normally takes place at a Sunday Eucharist. Whether it is celebrated at this time or at another celebration when a portion of the parish is gathered, various ministers are involved. Their specific preparation will depend on many variations according to the parish and liturgy in which the rite is celebrated. Consider the following ministries and the specific preparation needed to celebrate this rite well in your circumstances.

✧ **The presider, the liturgist, the music director, and the initiation coordinator** determine together specific choices regarding the celebration of the rite.

✧ The **sponsors** rehearse so as to be familiar with specific gestures, responses, and places within the worship space. The rehearsal generally occurs before the day of the rite.

✧ The **musicians and cantors** are familiar with any additional acclamations used and their placement in the liturgy.

✧ The **lectors** are informed of the readings to be proclaimed, well ahead of the day of the celebration. The one who reads the intercessions is familiar with the pronunciation of names of those for whom the community prays.

✧ The **eucharistic ministers** are given direction as to the flow of the distribution of communion so as to incorporate the reception of Eucharist by the newly-received candidate.

✧ The **ushers and greeters** are aware of the candidates' family and friends who need to be particularly welcomed and informed of seating possibilities.

Engaging the Assembly

The "Rite of Reception" is not a private experience. The parish community needs to be involved both in the formation of those preparing for this rite and in the celebration of the rite. In the preparation for and celebration of the "Rite of Reception," include some of the following ways of involving the parish community.

Preparation

✧ Invite the candidates, sponsors, and family members to join a small faith community.

✧ Invite small faith communities, prayer groups, liturgical ministers, and others who are interested to participate in the formation sessions.

✧ Invite the candidates, sponsors, and family members to come to various parish prayer and social action activities.

✧ Make the community aware of the candidates' journey to the Catholic faith through announcements in the newsletter, bulletin, introductions before and after Mass, and the intercessions.

✧ Invite the community, especially those who have shared in the formation of the candidates, to participate in the immediate spiritual preparation and mystagogy with the candidates.

Celebration of the Rite of Reception

✧ Publicize the date and time of the candidates' "Rite of Reception." Invite the community to share in the celebration.

✧ The week before the celebration of the rite, through the bulletin and announcements, invite the community to reflect on the journey shared by all Christians of living as baptized followers of Christ.

✧ Invite everyone—individually, as families, and at parish gatherings—to pray for the candidates being received.

✧ Prepare the gathered assembly through an announcement before the Mass begins and a rehearsal of musical acclamations to be used.

C. Preparing the Rite

Decisions That Need To Be Made

When to Celebrate the Rite?

Here are some considerations:

✧ The readiness of the candidates needs to be discerned. When they complete their catechetical formation, a date could be set for the rite and shared with the parish, and a time of spiritual preparation would then lead up to the celebration of the rite.

✧ The candidates to be received should be consulted about the celebration (RCIA 475.2), particularly about the question of whether there are pastoral reasons for celebrating with a smaller group. Ecumenical sensitivities should be respected in scheduling the celebration and signs of triumphalism avoided.

✧ Because Sunday Mass is the primary time when the community gathers, it would be the best occasion on which to celebrate the "Rite of Reception" with full communal support.

✧ Choosing a Sunday with appropriate readings is important. Many Sundays in Ordinary Time that bring forward themes of discipleship, as well as Sundays in the Easter season that tell the story of the growth of the Christian community, can be excellent choices. Lent is a season to be avoided because of its focus on the rites of purification and enlightenment.

✧ Reception can be celebrated as often as necessary during the year, but should not be celebrated so often that it becomes tedious for the Sunday assembly.

How Will We Highlight the Central Symbols?

Here are some ideas:

✧ While it is always helpful to have candidates visible, keep in mind that when they profess the creed, they do so as part of the assembly. A position in a central aisle or some area clearly part of the assembly is a good place from which to begin the rite.

✧ After the act of reception, the candidates might then change position, coming forward to face the assembly for the laying on of hands and the prayer of Confirmation. This movement forward would signal a new moment in the rite.

✧ One popular adaptation of the ritual of Confirmation is to have the assembly join in the extension of hands with the presider. This is a strong visual symbol of the support of the community. Because in this rite (unlike the celebration of the rite of Confirmation elsewhere) hands are laid on each candidate individually, the presider's role remains distinct.

✧ Music at the communion rite should accent the community dimension of Eucharist. Communion is always offered under both forms, at least to the newly-received and to those closest to them (RCIA 498).

How Will the Assembly Be Active and Involved?

Here are some ideas:

✧ A clear and enthusiastic introduction to this celebration should be included in the entrance rites at Mass. The candidates and their sponsors could walk in the entrance procession and be named in the opening words after the liturgical greeting.

✧ The introduction to the celebration of reception (RCIA 490) gives the presider freedom to adapt this text. After he invites the profession of faith, he might underline the role of the assembly in professing the creed with the candidates so that they do so with greater deliberateness and attention.

✧ Extension of hands at the prayer of Confirmation and participation in any music sung during the rite of Confirmation can help to engage the assembly in calling on the Spirit.

✧ While no particular role is scripted for the catechist, catechists are expected to take an active part in the rites (RCIA 16), and their visible presence affirms the variety of ministries in the community. They can assist in various ways, for example, calling forward the candidates by name, introducing their sponsors, bringing forward the sacred chrism for Confirmation, and so on.

D. After the Rite

Evaluation of the Rite of Reception

Take some time within ten days of celebrating the "Rite of Reception" to evaluate what went well, what did not, and what needs to be changed for the next celebration of this rite. Some people you may wish to involve in the evaluation are: the coordinator, the presider, the liturgist, the music director, and some additional team members. In addition to a core group of those who will reflect on the experience of this liturgy, input may be elicited from others in the parish.

A process similar to the one below may be helpful.

1. Evaluators reflect on their experiences, using the format on page 77 which may be duplicated as needed.
2. Each evaluator elicits responses from three parishioners who participated in this liturgy.
3. The evaluators come together to talk about their experiences and make appropriate suggestions for the next celebration of this (and possibly other) major rites.
4. The coordinator meets with appropriate persons to talk about these changes.

Evaluation: Rite of Reception into the Full Communion of the Catholic Church

The rite celebrated was: _____ The "Rite of Reception" within Mass

_____ The "Rite of Reception" outside Mass

Date of celebration _____ Time of celebration _____

Sunday of Church year _____ Weekday celebration _____ Number of those received into full communion _____

1. For me the highlight of the rite was _____

   because _____ .

2. For me the part of the rite that was least meaningful was _____

   because _____ .

3. If I were to describe the important parts of this rite to others, I would tell them _____

   _____ .

4. Rate the following on a scale of 1–10 (1 is low, 10 is high) on how well
   this part of the rite was celebrated and give a reason for your response.

   _____ The profession of faith _____

   _____ The act of reception _____

   _____ The sacrament of Confirmation _____

   _____ Eucharistic communion of the newly-received _____

   _____ The music that supported the liturgical action of the rite _____

   _____ The music that was sung well by the assembly _____

5. If I were to change something in how this rite is celebrated the next time, I would suggest _____

   _____

   because _____ .

6. Other details that need to be remembered for the next celebration of the "Rite of Reception" are: _____

   _____

   _____ .

Mystagogy

Gather the newly received and various other members of the community within a few days of the celebration. Specifically invite those who were part of the formation process, the choir, the musicians, the lectors, and the eucharistic ministers who were present at the celebration, as well as the assembly. The invitation to participate in this reflection on the rite is included in the parish bulletin when the date of the celebration of the "Rite of Reception" is published.

Reflecting on the Rite of Reception

Gathering

1. Gather in the worship space near the altar. Display the Easter candle lighted, a vessel of chrism, bread and wine. Or gather in another suitable space, using these sacramental symbols as part of the environment.

2. Welcome everyone. Invite the participants to stand as a group as you name each group: newly received into full communion, sponsors, family members, those who were part of the formation process, ministers at the celebration, and members of the assembly.

3. Give this introduction: *Tonight we gather in a special way with (names) who were received into the full communion of the Catholic Church only a few days ago. We ask them to share with us what they experienced in the "Rite of Reception," Confirmation, and Eucharist. We all share how God spoke to us at this celebration. Let us join together this night in the spirit of the living Body of Christ.*

4. Sing together "Gather Your People" (Hurd, OCP).

5. Pray this prayer: *Loving and gracious God, you have called us and formed us into the living Body of Christ. You have made us one in the Eucharist. You have made this community, your Church, fuller through the reception of our brothers and sisters (names) into the full communion of the Catholic Church. We give you thanks. Open our hearts and spirits to understand more fully your Spirit's presence in us as we gather in oneness at the Table of the Lord's Body and Blood. Inspire us this evening with the Spirit who hovers around us and breathes within us. We ask this through Christ, the One who shows us the way. Amen.*

Remembering

1. Invite everyone to reflect on their experience in this way: *Let's take a few moments to go inside ourselves and breathe. God's own Spirit breathes within us. Go back in time to when you first arrived at church for the "Rite of Reception." Recall gathering together, singing the hymn, and listening to God's Word to us.* (Insert some phrases both from the Scripture readings and the homily.) *(Names) made their profession of faith and were received into the full communion of the Catholic Church. They were sealed with fragrant chrism in Confirmation. All of us gathered as one baptized community around the Table of the Lord for the eucharistic prayer. (Names) ate and drank the Body and Blood of the Lord with us for the first time. This entire community, this living Body of Christ, was sent forth to live our Christian faith.*

2. Invite everyone, with their eyes still closed, to call out a word or phrase naming a part of this celebration that was powerful for them. Allow several minutes for these responses. When they are finished, ask people to open their eyes and return to this space.

3. Ask those who wish, beginning with those received and their sponsors, followed by family members and others in the assembly, to stand and share something of their experience at the "Rite of Reception."

4. Ask everyone to reflect on these four questions and share their responses in groups of three with the persons sitting around them. Hand these questions out on paper.

   From the "Rite of Reception":
   A. What does it mean to profess the Catholic faith?
   B. What experience of God's Spirit comes alive for you?
   C. What does it mean for us to eat together at the Table of the Lord's Body and Blood?
   D. Give some concrete examples of how sharing in the Eucharist calls us to be Christ's body in our world.

5. After about ten minutes, invite a sharing of responses to the questions in the large group one at a time.

Prayer

1. Invite everyone to stand around the altar.

2. Sing the refrain of "One Bread, One Body" (Foley, New Dawn Music).

3. Have a lector proclaim 1 Corinthians 12:4–13.

4. Ask those who wish to share a prayer aloud.

5. Give this invitation: *As the Body of Christ for the world, let us offer one another the peace of Christ. Share a sign of peace.*

PART THREE

The Minor Rites

✧ Rites Belonging to the
   Period of the Catechumenate

✧ Rites Belonging to the Period
   of Purification and Enlightenment

✧ The Rite of Dismissal

Rites Belonging to the Period of the Catechumenate

CELEBRATIONS OF THE WORD, MINOR EXORCISMS, BLESSINGS, ANOINTING WITH THE OIL OF CATECHUMENS

Understanding the Rites

The formation of the catechumenate period includes catechesis, community, liturgical rites, and apostolic works (RCIA 75). Indeed each of these four aspects of the period presumes the others, and all four are interrelated. The period of the catechumenate is to be richly colored by liturgical experience that will foster the spiritual growth of the catechumens, respond to their needs, and call them into an ever deeper experience of conversion that prepares them for mission. Woven into the fabric of the patient, day-to-day process of becoming a Christian are rites that instruct, edify, purify, bless, and strengthen those who are on this journey of faith. The Church "like a mother" (RCIA 75.3) ministers to the catechumens through these liturgical rites during the time of their formation.

The rites belonging to the period of the catechumenate stand out as the visible signs of the inner vitality of an emerging Christian—the heartbeat, the breathing, and the flow of blood of a new life. The more these rites are celebrated, the more the catechumen lives into a new identity.

Celebrations of the Word

To live the Christian way of life, catechumens must embrace the Word and, in turn, be embraced by it—not by an inert and lifeless word, but by the Word proclaimed and preached and sung, day-in and day-out, by a community of believers. In encountering the Word week by week (1) in the Sunday liturgy, (2) in Word services joined to catechetical sessions, and (3) in other "Celebrations of the Word" specially arranged for them, the catechumens truly come to meet the Word who is Christ.

"Celebrations of the Word" are the foremost rites of this period (RCIA 79). When such celebrations are held in conjunction with catechetical sessions or on other occasions outside of Sunday Mass, a priest, a deacon, or a catechist may preside and preach at them, provided he or she is capable and prepared. The celebrations should "accord with the liturgical season" (RCIA 81) and flow from the teachings that are being presented. A model for such celebrations is provided in RCIA 85–89.

Minor Exorcisms

It is likewise essential for the Christian to come to grips with the reality of evil on an everyday basis—to recognize and name its existence; but, more importantly, to rest in the confidence that through Christ the power of evil is broken and nothing can keep us from the beatitude of God's reign. The minor exorcisms purify the catechumens "little by little" (RCIA 75) and also teach them the necessity and importance of turning to God in prayer for deliverance from evil.

These exorcisms may be presided over by a priest, a deacon, or a catechist (RCIA 16). The diocesan bishop may give catechists a special deputation to preside at these minor exorcisms, but in the dioceses of the United States *all* catechists are deputed, unless a different policy exists in the local diocese. The minor exorcisms occur at the beginning or end of a catechetical session (similar to an opening or closing prayer), or in a "Celebration of the Word." The catechumens kneel or bow their heads, the presider extends hands over them and prays the prayer, adapting it as necessary. These prayers are rich in scriptural content and pastoral in nature. They may even be used one-to-one as needed. One enhancement of the rite would be to include any of the faithful who are present by also having them extend their hands or place their hands on the shoulders of the catechumens.

Blessings

If the minor exorcisms are the rites of purification of this period, emptying the person of deceits and casting out evil, the rite of blessing is a means of calling forth the fullness and abundance of God's gifts, filling up in the soul and treasuring in the heart what is truly of God and is therefore life-giving. A trusting openness to the loving God who cares for us is the indispensable attitude of a Christian that the "Rite of Blessing" teaches. A reliance upon God rather than our own resources is the key to this spiritual reality. The holiness of hunger and need and the experience of standing empty-handed before God are what the "Rite of Blessing" presumes in those it addresses.

Like the minor exorcisms, catechists may offer them as well as priests and deacons (see above). These blessings are offered in a standing posture, and the presider extends hands over those being blessed. This extension of hands is followed by the imposition of the presider's hands on the head of each catechumen. For a full expression of this gesture, both hands should be used; it should be a deliberate, unhurried movement. When the catechumens come forward one by one to receive this imposition of hands, the effect is somewhat like coming forward for communion, and indeed it is a kind of preparation for Eucharist in the broad sense. Again it is a good idea to include sponsors and others of the faithful who are present, perhaps by having them touch the catechumens or extend their hands over them with the presiding minister. Blessings take place either at the end of a celebration of the Word or the end of a catechetical session.

Anointing with the Oil of Catechumens

The reality of struggle in embracing the Christian life is acknowledged in the "Rite of Anointing with the Oil of Catechumens." The "two ways" spoken of in the ancient Church document, *Didache*—the way of life and the way of death—are ever present choices; and the decision to walk on the pathway of life is not easy. Anointing strengthens the catechumens in the struggle against evil, sin, and "the way of death." The symbolism of anointing is derived from the ancient practice of oiling the skin of athletes before a contest. Anointing with the oil of catechumens limbers the spiritual muscles of the catechumens so that they can hold fast to their profession of faith and, conversely, makes it difficult for Satan to grasp and hold onto them!

Anointing with the oil of catechumens may take place more than once to mark the progress of the catechumens on their journey. In other words, at certain intervals this rite is celebrated to encourage the catechumens to press onward— perhaps two or three times in the course of a year-long process. A priest or a deacon presides at this rite, which takes place in a celebration of the Word. Usually the oil blessed by the bishop at the Chrism Mass is used, but, for pastoral reasons, the oil may be blessed by a priest in the rite of anointing itself. The breast and hands are anointed and the anointing may be followed by a blessing.

Although these rites begin in the period of the catechumenate, all of them may continue to be celebrated through the period of purification and enlightenment as well.

Baptized Candidates: What's Different?

"Celebrations of the Word" nourish the faith of baptized candidates as much as that of the catechumens, and all should be included. Given the pastoral purposes of the blessings and minor exorcisms, and using the freedom of RCIA 407, it also makes sense to adapt these rites of blessing and purification for the benefit of the baptized candidates. The Canadian edition of the *Rite of Christian Initiation of Adults* contains specific texts adapted for the baptized.

Anointing with the oil of catechumens is a rite specific to catechumens, marking their distinctive journey in preparing for Baptism. The baptized candidates, therefore, should not be anointed. A blessing particularly for the baptized candidates might be offered in the same celebration however, if both candidates and catechumens are present.

Rites Belonging to the Period of Purification and Enlightenment

PRESENTATION OF THE CREED AND THE LORD'S PRAYER

Understanding the Presentations

The ritual text indicates that there are two presentation rites that belong to the period of purification and enlightenment. During this period, the presentation of the Creed follows the "First Scrutiny," which is celebrated on the Third Sunday of Lent; and the presentation of the Lord's Prayer follows the "Third Scrutiny," which is celebrated on the Fifth Sunday of Lent. These presentations are to be celebrated during the week following the celebration of the scrutiny—it is not to be incorporated into the same liturgy as the scrutiny.

The meaning of the presentations is explained in paragraphs 147–149 of the *Rite of Christian Initiation of Adults.* Having completed their catechetical formation, the Church entrusts the elect with these two treasures from the tradition—the Creed and the Lord's Prayer. These texts, which come down to us from the earliest times, express the heart of the Church's faith and prayer. Thus the elect are presented with the Creed and the Lord's Prayer

as a further enlightenment, almost as a capstone to the catechetical formation they received in the catechumenate.

It must be emphasized, however, that these presentations are not a handing on of a written text but the transmission of a lived tradition of a people who have placed their faith in God and called upon that same God in prayer for two thousand years. These presentations celebrate the essence of our relationship to God who calls us out of darkness and into light. They succinctly and powerfully express what we give ourselves over to, what we believe, and how we call upon God in prayer.

For most of the two thousand years of our history as a Church, the Creed and Lord's Prayer have been handed down by oral tradition—parent to child, one believer to the next. New members learned these texts from the lips of those who knew them by heart. This is why, for example, the rite stipulates that the elect are to commit the Creed to memory. The Creed and the Lord's Prayer must be considered living confessions that celebrate the heart and soul of one's relationship to God, nurtured in the community of the Church.

The Rite at a Glance: The Presentation of the Creed

LITURGY OF THE WORD

    Readings

    Homily

    Presentation of the Creed

    Prayer over the Elect

    Dismissal of the Elect

LITURGY OF THE EUCHARIST

Understanding the Presentation of the Creed

This first major element addressed in the ritual text is the choice of **readings.** The weekday readings are not used, and in their place, other readings are used (see RCIA 158). These Scripture readings emphasize the dynamic character of the presentation. The elect listen with their heart (Deuteronomy). This whole-hearted listening leads ultimately to a confession of faith or belief (Romans or First Corinthians) that is nurtured by the Church and by the One who is the Light of the world (Matthew or John).

The **homily** should not only draw upon the Scriptures; it should also refer to the Creed itself. The significance of this statement of our belief must be highlighted, especially in the light of the elect's long process of formation in the catechumenate. The tradition into which they have been immersed and the teaching of the Church that has been offered to them is summed up and symbolized in the Creed. The Creed is considered one of the four pillars that sustains the transmission of faith, along with the sacraments, the Ten Commandments, and the Lord's Prayer. The homily may make mention of the fact that the Creed, which the elect now receive, will be recited back by them (if this is included in the "Preparation Rites" of Holy Saturday).

After the homily, an **invitation** is made to the elect to come forward. Paragraph 160 of the Rite indicates that a deacon or another assisting minister, such as the director of initiation, a catechist, or one of the team members, makes this invitation. The elect should be accompanied by their godparents. The elect come forward and then they are instructed to listen carefully and receive what they are hearing with an open heart. Once the invitation and this instruction have been completed, the elect should then face either the whole assembly or a section of the assembly of the faithful, depending on the worship space. To highlight their receptivity, the elect could be prompted by their godparents to extend their hands out, palms up, in a gesture of receiving a gift.

For the **presentation,** either the Apostles' Creed or the Nicene Creed are to be presented. The assembly slowly and reverently professes the faith of the Church in the words of the Creed. The elect listen carefully to this presentation. The three major sections of the Creed could serve as a natural break at which an acclamation that speaks of belief is sung, such as Marty Haugen's "We Remember" (GIA Publications) or one from the parish's musical repertoire.

After the Creed is received, a **prayer over the elect** is made. This consists of an invitation by the presider, some time for silence, and finally the prayer itself. During this prayer the entire assembly might be invited by the presider to extend hands over the elect. If the candidates are also a part of this rite (see RCIA 407), the prayer must be adapted since it refers to Baptism.

Once the prayer is concluded, the **dismissal of the elect** takes place, if Eucharist is to be celebrated. If the "Presentation of the Creed" has been celebrated in the context of a liturgy of the Word, then the entire assembly is dismissed at this time by the presider.

An Option for Celebrating the Rite: Consider the Setting

If the group gathered is small, perhaps the "Presentation of the Creed" could be celebrated in a more intimate setting other than in a large worship space. Perhaps in this smaller group setting two circles could be formed—the elect on the inside facing out and the godparents and team in the outer circle facing in toward the elect. The people in the outer circle would take the hands of the elect as they "hand" over to them the spoken words of the Creed. Again stop to punctuate the words with an acclamation.

The Rite at a Glance: Presentation of the Lord's Prayer

LITURGY OF THE WORD

    Readings

    Gospel Reading (Presentation of the Lord's Prayer)

    Homily

    Prayer over the Elect

    Dismissal of the Elect

LITURGY OF THE EUCHARIST

Understanding the Presentation of the Lord's Prayer

The rubrics indicate (RCIA 179) that in place of the regular weekday **readings** other readings are assigned from Hosea, Romans (or Galatians). These special readings emphasize how God leads us (Hosea), how we have receive the Spirit of adoption so that we cry out "Abba, Father" (Romans or Galatians). Clearly these Scriptures set the stage for the handing on of the Lord's Prayer by highlighting the divine initiative in making us children of our heavenly Father.

These texts are about our identity *vis-a-vis* God. The Lord makes us his own, part of his family. The Scriptures emphasize relationship, a closeness and oneness with the Lord of love and life, our shepherd, kind parent, who pours into our hearts the everlasting Spirit.

What distinguishes the structure of the **presentation** of the Lord's Prayer from the presentation of the Creed is that there is no particular additional text that is handed on to the elect. What is handed on in this presentation is the gospel pericope itself, the Lord's Prayer. The presider instructs the elect to listen carefully to the way in which the Lord Jesus teaches us to pray. Then the Gospel is proclaimed and the elect cherish it in their hearts. It is possible to distinguish this gospel proclamation by chanting it. However the celebrant must prepare ahead of time and understand that the text of the Lord's Prayer as given in the Gospel is not precisely the same as that which the assembly prays prior to receiving Communion. Therefore while the celebrant may already know the chant version sung during the communion rite, he will have to adapt this gospel proclamation because of its different wording.

The **homily** will clarify for the elect the preeminent place the Lord's Prayer has in the life of the community and in each of its members. We have been taught this prayer by the Lord Jesus himself. Boldly we dare to call on God as God's children. The Lord's Prayer summarizes the whole of the Good News, the Gospel, in that we can confidently approach the Father and ask in prayer what we need. All of us have particular petitions that we wish to bring before the Lord. The text of the Lord's Prayer sets the groundwork for our making those petitions. We know that God will respond to all our needs. The importance of this special prayer, handed on by the community in this rite, is underscored by the fact that the *Catechism of the Catholic Church* devotes a significant number of paragraphs to its explanation (2759–2865).

After the homily, the celebrant makes the **prayer over the elect.** While he holds his hands outstretched over them, he may invite the entire assembly to join him in this gesture. If for pastoral reasons (see RCIA 407) some or all of the candidates are also included in this rite, adaptation of this prayer must be made since it specifically refers to the elect and Baptism.

Finally, the **dismissal** is made. Options are provided for the elect to leave the assembly or to stay—even though they will not fully participate in the celebration of the Eucharist.

An Option for Celebrating the Rite: Consider the Setting

If the catechumenal community observes an extended retreat or day of recollection prior to initiation, for example, a weekend in Lent, the "Presentation of the Lord's Prayer" might be celebrated at this time. Given the nature of a retreat as a time of intense prayer, this rite may best be celebrated in the context of a "time away."

B. Preparing the Community

Preparing the Community for the Presentation of the Creed

The Creed, of course, is recited by the assembly every Sunday and major feast day. Because of this regular recitation, its words may have actually become too familiar, if that is possible. How many understand that the words of the Creed represent the baptismal promises of the faithful? We vow to be faithful to the Triune God who calls us into a life of community, love, and holiness—into the very life of the Trinity.

Scheduling the Presentation of the Creed

No matter whether a decision has been made to celebrate the presentation of the Creed at a Sunday Mass during the catechumenate period, a weekday Mass after the "First Scrutiny," or at a Liturgy of the Word, a good number of those who are fully initiated should be encouraged to attend. Obviously, Sunday Mass holds out the best possibility for this to be realized. But efforts can be made to bring together the community at times other than the celebration of Sunday Mass.

Perhaps during the week after the celebration of the "First Scrutiny," the parish will be holding a Lenten activity or event that would lend itself as a context for the "Presentation of the Creed." Or perhaps the community gathering to prepare for the "Second Scrutiny" would lend itself as a context for this presentation.

Catechetical and Spiritual Preparation of the Elect

No doubt the elect, during their formation in the period of the catechumenate, will have examined the Creed. John Paul II has written about the importance of the Creed as a major element in the expression of the living heritage of the Church's faith (*Catechesi Tradendae* 28). He suggests greater use be made of the Creed in adapted forms and in a variety of ways to heighten the elect's appreciation of the Creed as a symbol of our faith.

Here are some suggestions to prepare for the presentation:
- ✧ Encourage the elect to choose one of the phrases or sentences of the Creed and to ponder what it means to them. They would then share with the whole group.
- ✧ Ask the elect to paraphrase the text of the Nicene Creed or the Apostles' Creed in their own words.

Invite each person to write their own creed. Gather around the baptismal font and take turns praying the creed that each has formulated. A variation would be to invite each person to pray one line (sentence) of their creed, continuing around the circle until each person's entire creed has been prayed. Conclude by singing an acclamation.

Sample Bulletin Announcement for the Presentation of the Creed

Prior to the celebration of the "Presentation of the Creed," a bulletin article would benefit the entire community and the elect as they prepare for this important celebration. The parish would adapt the following text for its own purposes and include the details of when and where the presentation would be celebrated.

Our parish will celebrate the "Presentation of the Creed" *(time, place)*. In this celebration our elect will receive from us this important profession of the faith. We will recite the words of the Creed and they will listen. In turn, they will make this same profession of faith as they gather before the font to be baptized.

What does the Church say about the profession of faith? A creed concisely states the most central beliefs held by an individual or a community. The two creeds most widely accepted by Christians and upheld by the Catholic Church begin with the words "I believe" and "We believe." The formulation of the beliefs of the Church has come down to us from early Christian times in the text of the Apostles' Creed and the Nicene-Constantinopolitan Creed which express in concise, accepted, and approved language the central tenets of the faith.

This faith is only possible because of God's self-revelation to humanity. We in turn respond with an articulation of praise and thanksgiving as our search for ultimate meaning finds its fulfillment in God.

The term *creed* derives from the Latin *credo,* which means "to put one's heart into something" or "to give oneself to someone or something." Professing the Creed implies commitment. The Creed is an act of praise and thanksgiving by which we confess before God and one another what God has done and is doing for us through Christ and by the power of the Holy Spirit.

Faith, by its very nature, is meant to be active. Our response to God's revelation issues forth in Christian activity that seeks to pursue the holiness of God and prepare this world for the fullness of the kingdom. Catholics do not believe in the formulas themselves but in the realities they symbolize. The formulations of the Creed enable us to express faith, assimilate it, celebrate it, live it, and hand it on to others. This handing on of the faith is assisted by what we will do as a parish when we celebrate the "Presentation of the Creed" to the elect.

Preparing the Community for the Presentation of the Lord's Prayer

The Lord's Prayer is recited by the assembly of the faithful prior to every reception of the Eucharist. The initiation team could remind the assembly that the elect will soon receive this prayer. Invite everyone to pray the Lord's Prayer daily on behalf of the elect.

Catechetical and Spiritual Preparation of the Elect

The instruction provided by the *Catechism of the Catholic Church* on the various lines of the Lord's Prayer may be summarized and presented to the elect. In addition, a catechist or facilitator might work with the elect in preparation for the celebration of this rite by:

✧ Emphasizing the personal ("Father") and communal ("*Our* Father," "forgive us *our* trespasses as we forgive those who trespass against *us*") aspects of the prayer, and eliciting their response to this duality expressed in the prayer.

✧ Asking the elect how their prayer life has intensified at this stage in the initiation process, and inviting them to share on this.

Sample Bulletin Announcement for the Presentation of the Lord's Prayer

This sample could be adapted to your parish community in preparation for the celebration of the "Presentation of the Lord's Prayer."

Our elect will soon receive from us the prayer that summarizes the whole Gospel, the Lord's Prayer. We pray the Lord's Prayer as a community every weekday and Sunday before we partake of the Lord's meal, the Eucharist. What is it that we express in this prayer given to us by Jesus? Everything.

Saint Thomas Aquinas says that the Lord's Prayer is the most perfect of all prayers and in it we ask for all the things that we can properly desire. Just as Jesus' teaching on the Sermon on the Mount is teaching for life, so too the Lord's Prayer is a *prayer* for life.

The Lord's Prayer is so important that the early Christians prayed it three times daily. But it is not just a prayer text for individuals. It is prayed by the whole community together as evidenced by its first word: "Our." Even when the Lord's Prayer is prayed by an individual believer, it evokes the community in the use of that little word *our*. By praying the Lord's Prayer, one offers petitions on behalf of the whole household of the faithful.

The Lord's Prayer is the prayer of Jesus, the faithful and only begotten Son of the Father. It is the prayer of the disciples who are adopted into the family of faith. It is our prayer, the heartfelt raising of our minds and spirits to the One who shepherds us, loves us, and adopts us.

Decisions That Need to Be Made

The structure and flow of the two presentations are deceptively simple. There is not much detail to them and they are relatively easy to celebrate. It is more important that a faith community actually hand on the Creed and the Lord's Prayer in these celebrations rather than to do fancy things or augment the ritual as given. However there are various questions to consider prior to celebrating these liturgies.

When to Celebrate the Presentations?

Here are some considerations:

During Lent

✧ The rubrics clearly prefer that the presentations take place during the period of purification and enlightenment. These rituals are intended as loving events of "enlightenment" (RCIA 147) for those who have completed their catechetical formation.

✧ The presentations normally would be celebrated at a weekday Mass when at least some of the faithful can be present. In parishes where weekday Mass is not celebrated, a service of the Word or communion service involving the faithful would fulfill the same function.

✧ Another possibility might be to celebrate one of the presentations in the context of a parish retreat, keeping in mind the priority the rite places on celebrating the presentations as public, communal events.

✧ One pastoral strategy for celebrating the presentations during Lent might be to couple them with a renewal event open to the all the faithful as part of the Lenten program of the parish. Invite the parish to join with the elect in reflecting on these great treasures of our tradition, then go into the church and celebrate the rite.

✧ Another strategy is to link the presentations to community building. Following the weekday Mass at which a presentation takes place, hold a potluck supper and encourage some faith sharing among those who attend.

✧ Yet another approach would be to involve the bishop, perhaps celebrating the presentations at a deanery level.

Remind your local bishop that the *Ceremonial of Bishops* (CB) makes a particular point of urging bishops to celebrate the presentations (CB 421) because of the bishop's role as teacher and chief catechist of the diocese. Bishops may only do so, however, if the presentations are celebrated after the "Rite of Election."

Anticipating the Presentations

✧ Although a Lenten setting is preferred, the presentations may be celebrated earlier during the period of the catechumenate (RCIA 147). Pastoral necessity would prompt this earlier celebration. The Rite, however, does not specify precisely what pastoral reasons would cause the parish to anticipate the normative time of their celebration. Presumably the motivation would be to lighten the Lenten agenda (RCIA 104), to give the presentations greater prominence, celebrating them on a Sunday, and to give more time and attention to the catechetical preparation and reflection that might accompany them. In addition the presentation of the Lord's Prayer can also be deferred until the preparation rites of Holy Saturday (RCIA 149, 185).

✧ There are several complications that arise when the presentations are anticipated. One pastoral problem associated with celebrating the presentation of the Creed and the Lord's Prayer during the catechumenate period is the attendant uncertainty regarding for whom it is celebrated. The elect have not yet been discerned. Therefore it is an open question who will go on at this particular Easter to celebrate the initiation sacraments. This means that all catechumens—regardless of whether they will stay within the catechumenate for another year—receive the presentations. Yet the presentations should be experienced "[w]hen the formation of catechumens has been completed or is sufficiently far advanced . . ." (CB 420). "[T]he presentations are not to take place until a point during the catechumenate when the catechumens are judged ready for these celebrations" (RCIA 104).

✧ Another problem presents itself with regard to anticipating the presentation of the Lord's Prayer during the catechumenate period. This involves the choice of Scriptures. Since the Lord's Prayer is presented in the gospel reading itself, it would be necessary to celebrate this presentation on a Sunday when the Lectionary offers this reading. This restriction narrows the choices considerably (see page 88).

◇ Overall, it would seem better to present both the Creed and the Lord's Prayer during the period of purification and enlightenment. This is a heightened time, a retreat time for both the faith community at large and the elect themselves to prepare for the celebration of the initiation sacraments, and as such, this time is appropriate for the handing on of this symbol of the faith (Creed) and this summary of the Gospel (Lord's Prayer).

If the presentation of the Creed is anticipated during the catechumenate period, it would most likely take place on a Sunday when the whole community is gathered. The assigned readings from the Sunday lectionary cycle are used, and the suggestions given in paragraph 158 of the Rite are not. Some Sunday readings that might appropriately set the context for such a celebration would be:

Ordinary Time Sundays Appropriate to Celebrate the Presentation of the Creed

14th Sunday A—The readings refer to Father, Son and Spirit (the three parts of the Creed) and because the Gospel itself refers to the yoke of Jesus which is the new law of belief, as opposed to the old law of the Pharisees.

14th Sunday B—The gospel text refers to a lack of faith that the Church, in her profession of the Creed, now provides.

16th Sunday C—Jesus admonishes Martha, inviting her to be like Mary, sitting at the feet of the Lord who teaches us, gives us the better part, like the Creed.

17th Sunday A—The pearl of great price is like the Creed.

18th Sunday C—Those who are rich in the eyes of God would be the ones who profess faith.

20th Sunday C—The division Jesus speaks of is sometimes engendered by one's profession of the faith.

21 Sunday A—The keys to the kingdom open by professing faith.

23 Sunday B—Jesus opens our ears and mouths through the Creed.

Ordinary Time Gospel Texts of the Lord's Prayer

17th Sunday, C (Lectionary 111) Luke's version (nothing in the Lectionary with Matthew's version of the Lord's Prayer). In addition, there is only one weekday gospel reading that proclaims the Lord's Prayer, namely, Wednesday of the 27th week of the year, Year I (Lectionary 463).

To Whom Are the Creed and the Lord's Prayer Presented?

Here are some considerations:

◇ In addition to the elect and the unbaptized, it is possible that the Creed and the Lord's Prayer might be presented to uncatechized candidates. Baptized, uncatechized candidates may be presented with the Creed and the Lord's Prayer (RCIA 407), if the presentations suitably address their particular condition and spiritual needs.

◇ The situation of each candidate would need to be assessed by the team, a spiritual director, or the candidate's sponsor in order to determine whether both or either of the presentations is made to them along with the elect. Those who are assessing the candidates would need to determine if they have sufficient familiarity with the Creed and the Lord's Prayer. Have they used these hallowed texts in their practice of faith up to this point? By their noninclusion in one or both of these presentations these candidates would feel bereft in their formation toward full initiation and communion.

Which Text Is Used in the Presentations?

Here are some considerations:

◇ In presenting the **Creed,** two options are possible, namely, the Nicene-Constantinopolitan or the Apostles' Creed. Realize, however, that in presenting the Apostles' Creed, a text that is not normally professed on Sundays by the worshiping assembly, the impact of the rite may be diluted. While the Apostles' Creed is the more ancient text and a so-called baptismal creed, it is not the liturgical text used on Sundays. In addition the Nicene-Constantinopolitan Creed is an ecumenical creed; the Apostles' Creed is a Roman creed.

◇ In presenting the **Lord's Prayer,** the text given is found in Matthew's Gospel (according to the rubric in RCIA 180). However, the Lectionary indicates that in the presentation of the Lord's Prayer, two texts are possible, either Matthew 6:9–13 or Luke 11:1–2, even though only Matthew's version is printed in the Lectionary and the ritual text.

Note that Luke's version is significantly different from Matthew's: it does not begin with "our" Father and it is much shorter and more concise. Perhaps for this reason the framers of the ritual text reproduced Matthew's as the preferred text to be presented.

D. After the Rite of Presentation

Mystagogy on the Presentation of the Creed

As with all of the rites, it would be important to reflect with the elect upon their experience of the liturgy itself in order to savor it, draw out its meaning, and further apply it as they prepare for the initiation sacraments.

Mystagogical Reflection on the Rite

A catechist or a facilitator may want to spend time with the elect and ask them to reflect upon the celebration itself. After helping them to recall the various elements, or parts, of the liturgy, leading statements could assist the elect in processing this rite. Here are some suggestions:

- ✧ As I listened to the Creed, what stirred within me was . . .
- ✧ Having celebrated this rite, I learned . . .
- ✧ The assembly of the faithful handed the Creed on to me, and yet, I still have the following questions . . .

Evaluation

After the rite and indeed after the mystagogical reflection by the elect, the team may want to evaluate the celebration to determine its effectiveness. Here are some suggested questions to guide the evaluation:

- ✧ What worked in the celebration of the rite?
- ✧ Did we need better preparation? Why or why not?
- ✧ What didn't work in the celebration of the rite?
- ✧ How can we improve next time?

Mystagogy on the Presentation of the Lord's Prayer

The team may want to evaluate what happened during this presentation. Consider the following:

- ✧ Was the celebration itself prayerful? Why or why not?
- ✧ What do we want to retain next time that was effective?
- ✧ What do we want to modify because it was ineffective?

In addition having participated in the celebration of the rite, a catechist or a facilitator might help the elect further savor the experience and open up for themselves an appreciation of what is being handed on in this liturgy. For example:

- ✧ Invite them to share what stirred within them as they listened to the proclamation of the Gospel (the Lord's Prayer).
- ✧ Ask them to specifically ponder the text of the Lord's Prayer, reflecting on what it reveals about us as a Church, a community of love and justice.
- ✧ Invite them to listen to their godparents once again as their godparents pray the prayer and ask the elect what one word or phrase most speaks to them now and why.

PREPARATION RITES ON HOLY SATURDAY

Celebrating the Rites

The "Preparation Rites on Holy Saturday" are found in the ritual text, *The Rite of Christian Initiation of Adults* in paragraphs 185–205. These rites indicate the final rituals to be celebrated with the elect and are an immediate preparation for initiation at the Easter Vigil. As indicated in the introductory paragraphs of the ritual text, the elect are encouraged to spend Holy Saturday as a day of prayer and reflection in anticipation of their initiation that evening. Several rituals are provided for such a gathering of the elect. A model for celebrating these rituals is indicated in paragraphs 187–192.

When Are These Rituals Celebrated?

The most opportune time to celebrate these rituals is on Holy Saturday. If possible, the whole day could be set aside as a day of prayer and reflection. An extended celebration of the Word, inclusive of the various rituals, would prepare the elect for their initiation that evening at the Vigil. If setting aside the whole day is not possible, then the following could be considered:

- ✧ A half day of prayer and reflection that would include a celebration of the Word and the "Preparation Rites."
- ✧ An extended celebration of the Word (an hour or so) that would include the "Preparation Rites."
- ✧ The "Preparation Rites" in conjunction with the parish celebration of the Liturgy of the Hours on Holy Saturday morning.
- ✧ The "Preparation Rites" celebrated on another day and time—within the week—that gathers the elect for preparation for the Vigil.

Who Celebrates These Rituals?

The elect, their godparents, their spouses, the members of the team, the presider, the ministers for the Vigil, and other members of the parish are invited and encouraged to participate in the celebration of the "Preparation Rites." If the presider for the Vigil is present, he would be the celebrant for this rite. If he cannot be present, perhaps a deacon can preside. If neither the priest nor the deacon can be present, then the director of the parish initiation process is encouraged to lead the celebration.

Where Are the Preparation Rites Celebrated?

Consider using a space that affords a quiet and prayerful atmosphere. If the space where the Easter Vigil will be celebrated is in readiness for the Vigil, that space would be most appropriate for this celebration. However, if the space is in the process of being prepared, then another space needs to be chosen. Some parishes choose to go to a retreat center for this celebration. Others may choose to use a room or space at the parish that is conducive to prayer. Whatever space is chosen, set an environment for prayer that would include a focus point, such as a candle, the Lectionary or Bible opened to the chosen readings, a white cloth, and so on.

What Format Is Used?

In RCIA 187–192 a model format is indicated for the celebration of these "Preparation Rites." It is a celebration of the Word, which includes the "Preparation Rites" chosen prior to the celebration. The readings need to be chosen and prepared ahead of time. The number of readings would be determined in conjunction with the decision about which rites are to be celebrated. A gospel passage is the only reading needed. However, there are several other readings suggested. The team, along with the presider, determines the reading(s).

Which Rites to Celebrate?

- ✧ Recitation of the Creed
  This rite is an immediate preparation for the elect and candidates who will make their profession of faith at the Vigil. If the community has celebrated the "Presentation of the Creed" (RCIA 157–163), then this rite would be celebrated. It would not be celebrated if the "Presentation of the Creed" was not celebrated. The presider for the celebration of the "Presentation of the Creed" would also normally be the presider for the "Recitation of the Creed." Note that RCIA 196 indicates that the form of the Creed that was presented is also the Creed that is "handed back" in this recitation.

- ✧ Ephphetha Rite
  This rite is a simple but powerful ritual that prepares the elect not only to receive the Word of God but also to be

willing to proclaim "from the rooftops" the Word of God, which has taken root within their minds and hearts. If this rite is celebrated, it should be celebrated first—before the "Recitation of the Creed." Baptized candidates could also celebrate this ritual since in the *Rite of Baptism for Children* it is celebrated after Baptism. The precedent is set to be inclusive of those who have been baptized whether as infants or adults. It is encouraged to use the same gesture that was used to do the signings found in the "Rite of Acceptance."

✧ **Choosing a Baptismal Name**
This rite is not to be confused with the *Rite of Confirmation* at which confirmandi might choose a name. Note the introductory paragraph of the ritual text (RCIA 33.4), which indicates that for the United States there is to be no giving of a new name unless such a decision is made by the local ordinary. As RCIA 200 and 202 indicate, this rite can be used as a Christian interpretation and celebration of the elect's given name.

✧ **Presentation of the Lord's Prayer**
In RCIA 149 there is an indication that the Lord's Prayer could be deferred until the time of the celebration of the "Preparation Rites on Holy Saturday." Unless there is a very serious reason to defer the "Presentation of Lord's Prayer," it is strongly recommended that it not be included with the "Preparation Rites on Holy Saturday."

✧ **Anointing with the Oil of Catechumens**
Note that RCIA 33.7 indicates that the "Anointing with the Oil of Catechumens" is to be carried out at a time distinct and separate from the "Preparation Rites on Holy Saturday."

Baptized Candidates

Which of these "Preparation Rites" do we celebrate with baptized candidates? If there are candidates for reception into full communion who will make their profession of faith at the Easter Vigil, they would be encouraged to join the elect on Holy Saturday for the celebration of the "Preparation Rites" and for the time of prayer and reflection. Likewise, any Catholic candidates who will complete their Christian initiation at the Easter Vigil with Confirmation and Eucharist would join with others in this time of prayerful preparation. As indicated in RCIA 407, they may benefit from some of the rites provided for the unbaptized; but care must be exercised so that the language of the prayers respect their status as baptized members of the faith.

Music Suggestions

✧ Appendix Two of the rite indicates acclamations, hymns, and songs that would be most appropriate for the celebration of the "Preparation Rites."

✧ Acclamations that have been sung throughout the initiation process would also be appropriate, especially those used during the "Rite of Acceptance" and the rites of dismissal.

✧ Refrains from the Iona Community (GIA Publications), such as "If You Believe and I Believe" or Marty Haugen's "We Remember" (GIA Publications) are also appropriate.

✧ Caution: this is not the time to introduce new music to the elect.

Other Observations

✧ Do not omit the "Preparation Rites." They provide a needed means of immediate prayer and preparation for the elect and the candidates. It is important that advance preparation be done by the presider and the team so that they have a time to be present with and to the elect and the candidates.

✧ This is not a rehearsal time for the Vigil. A rehearsal with godparents and sponsors and team can be carried out at a time separate from the celebration of the "Preparation Rites."

✧ Encourage the elect, the candidates, the godparents, and the sponsors to refrain from usual activities. This is a day to vigil—to anticipate the great celebration of the Easter Vigil and their full initiation into the Catholic way of life. Give advance notice of this day and its purpose and the celebration of the "Preparation Rites." Many need this notice in order to arrange to take the necessary time to be present for the day as well as to make their own home preparations for the celebration of Easter.

Rite of Dismissal

Ancient Roots

Pre-Vatican II Catholics remember when the first part of the Mass, which we now call the Liturgy of the Word, was referred to as the Mass of the Catechumens. Similarly what we now call the Liturgy of the Eucharist was known as the Mass of the Faithful. These designations reflected the ancient practice of the Church of dismissing catechumens from the assembly after the homily while the "faithful" (the baptized) remained for the eucharistic prayer. The origins of such a practice are related to what is termed the *disciplina arcani,* or "discipline of the secret." This was a custom, observed especially in the fourth century, of withholding from those under instruction certain details of the Church's ritual practice and beliefs surrounding the sacraments. Partly in imitation of the pagan mystery cults that withheld details of their initiation rites, and partly out of a sense that the unbaptized were simply unable to grasp the full meaning of the sacramental mysteries prior to their actually experiencing them, those responsible for the initiation process did not reveal to catechumens in detail just what happened in the second half of the Mass.

An Ancient Practice Renewed

When the *Rite of Christian Initiation of Adults* reintroduced the dismissal of catechumens as a normal feature of the initiation process, many commentators rejected the idea as an unrealistic pastoral suggestion and a meaningless relic of the past. Nonetheless the ritual text says that catechumens are "normally dismissed" prior to the general intercessions and Creed. But the text quickly adds, "the group of catechumens goes out but does not disperse. With the help of some of the faithful, the catechumens remain together to share their joy and spiritual

experiences" (RCIA 67). As if to reinforce the point that a dismissal is the expected norm, the Rite goes on to indicate that if the catechumens remain for the Liturgy of the Eucharist, it should only be "for serious reasons" (RCIA 67).

The implementation of the Rite in the last twenty-five years has witnessed an evolution of pastoral practice in regard to the matter of the "Rite of Dismissal." Initially very few communities attempted to implement this aspect of the pastoral norms on a regular basis. Some tried it on a limited basis, particularly during the season of Lent, and as they did so, more and more communities began to recognize its value and incorporate a rite of dismissal into the regular pattern of their Sunday celebrations throughout the year. Although there is no hard data on how widespread this practice is today, anecdotal evidence suggests that a substantial number of parishes in the United States regularly dismiss those in the catechumenate from the Sunday assembly prior to the profession of faith, spending time thereafter in a catechetical session focused on the Liturgy of the Word just celebrated.

Discovering the Many Pastoral Benefits of the Dismissal

How is one to explain the phenomenon of an apparently unrealistic and outdated relic of the past becoming normative practice in so short a period of time, even though it remains an optional element of the rite? The answer lies in the considerable pastoral value that those who have "tried it out" have discovered in implementing the "Rite of Dismissal." Initiatory catechesis is preeminently liturgical in character, and the "Dismissal"allows catechists to maintain a close continuity with the liturgical experience of the larger assembly and to engage in reflection on the Sunday readings and homily in a very natural fashion. Far from feeling "kicked out," as many feared would be the reaction of those dismissed, catechumens who are dismissed consistently describe their experience as one of being cared for and having special attention lavished on them. In the experience of those dismissed, St. Augustine's description of the Liturgy of the Word as a table from which catechumens are fed—in parallel to the eucharistic table from which the faithful are fed—has become a lived reality, rather than mere poetic expression. The fact that catechumens are dismissed also highlights for them—and for the rest of the assembly—the fact that initiation is all about a process aimed at participation in the Liturgy of the Eucharist. Anthropologists refer to a "liminal period" in rites of passage, a time in-between, a period when the one being initiated is no longer what she or he used to be, but still not yet what she or he will become. Many have noted that the dismissal is a powerfully expressive liminal ritual that reminds the entire community, as well as those dismissed, that while they are in the process of coming to membership, there is still something lacking that keeps them from being full members. In such a situation, there is a gradual increase in their longing to be fully incorporated, a longing to be one at the Table of Eucharist with the larger assembly of believers. The ritual of dismissal is thus a very forceful way of catechizing the larger community, as well as the catechumens, about the connection between Baptism and Eucharist.

What About the Candidates?

This raises the question in many people's minds of whether it is fitting to dismiss baptized candidates together with the catechumens. Because of their Baptism, candidates have a place in the eucharistic assembly. They may share in praying the eucharistic prayer with the faithful, even though they do not yet take Communion. For catechized candidates especially, dismissal may be inappropriate. In many cases, however, pastoral practice has shown that the already baptized can and do profit just as much from the "Rite of Dismissal" as do their unbaptized counterparts. This is especially true of the uncatechized candidates. As a matter of fact, the candidates are excluded from eucharistic participation even if they remain in the liturgical assembly. Many people feel that inviting them to feast on the Word of God with the catechumens is actually a more hospitable practice than having them remain with the faithful and be refused participation in Holy Communion. When those candidates who for many years have worshiped with a Catholic spouse are first told that they will be dismissed, they often resist. However, when asked to "try it out" for a while, they almost always resolve to continue being dismissed and participate in the dismissal catechesis with the rest of the catechumenal group.

How to Celebrate the Dismissal

The "Rite of Dismissal" takes place after the homily when a moment of silence has settled and before the assembly rises for the profession of faith and general intercessions. If there is a deacon, the deacon would call the catechumens up and send them forth; but the presiding priest would probably speak to them briefly before they go, enjoining them to open the riches of the Word of God and reminding them of their special place in the prayers and concern of the whole community. If there is no deacon, the catechumens are dismissed by the presider.

There are various ways to celebrate the "Rite of Dismissal." Some parishes have the catechumens and candidates stand wherever they are in the church, and they are sent forth from their places. Others call the catechumens and candidates forward as a group, and their departure from the assembly takes on more of the appearance of a procession, led by the catechist who will conduct the dismissal catechesis. Other communities have experimented with calling forward catechumens and candidates in two different groups, to show their differing baptismal status.

The words spoken in the dismissal should be warm—the rite indicates that the catechumens are "kindly dismissed"—but the words should be brief. This is not an occasion for the use of the blessings or minor exorcisms or the laying on of hands, nor is it a time to give a recap of the homily. Dismissal is a brief pastoral moment in the liturgy, acknowledging the presence of catechumens and candidates in the midst of the assembly and sending them forth with grace and dignity. A ritual conclusion to whatever words of dismissal are offered, such as "Go in peace," can be an opportunity for the catechumens to become comfortable with the common liturgical response well known to Catholics, "Thanks be to God!"

As a general rule, the movement of groups of people in the liturgy usually is accompanied by music, and the dismissal would be no exception. Any music used should be simple and unobtrusive. Instrumental music or a seasonal acclamation to accompany the dismissal can help to integrate the dismissal into the overall unfolding of the service, avoiding self-consciousness on the part of the catechumens and candidates.

Because the dismissal catechesis will reflect on the Scripture readings that were proclaimed in the liturgy, many communities have developed the practice of having the catechist carry aloft the Lectionary as she or he leads the catechumens out of the assembly. (The Gospel Book remains in the sanctuary.) When a catechist comes forward to lead the catechumens in the dismissal, it may be a good idea to have someone, for example, the presider, hand the Lectionary to the catechist. Regularity and repetition will help this movement to flow smoothly.

APPENDIX

Making the Transition to Baptism by Immersion

In many ways the *Rite of Christian Initiation of Adults* proposes a vigorous renewal of the Church's practices of initiation. The catechumenal process envisioned is multifaceted and community-based, it takes place over a substantial period of time, and the liturgical rites that punctuate it are robust, memorable, formative events.

Nowhere is the call to a renewed experience of the liturgies of initiation so evident as in the Rite's preference for Baptism by immersion. Reaching back into the ancient practice of the Church, the Rite proposes immersion as the first choice, the preferred means of Baptism, and only then does it also mention the pouring of water as an option. The National Statutes call Baptism by immersion "the fuller and more expressive sign of the sacrament" (RCIA, NS 17), and its alternative is not the sprinkling of a few drops of water, but partial immersion or "immersion of the head" (RCIA, NS 17).

Many older churches are poorly equipped for Baptism by immersion. Fonts consisting of a small basin, from which to pour a small amount of water on the head of a small baby, are frequently tucked away in a small baptismal chapel, for the family that would be present. Clearly these fonts, which served in a different day and age, were constructed with a minimalist view of Baptism. Communities that worship in such churches must be creative in adapting their main worship space for adult Baptism at the Vigil, until such time as a renovation can be brought about. New and renovated churches are generally equipped with a font large enough to immerse an adult.

Why Baptize by Immersion?

Sacraments are meant to engage our senses. Through the actions and the material elements of the liturgy, we encounter in a transforming way the grace of God's presence and activity in our lives. When we use robust symbols, we provide for a more fruitful experience of the sacraments. Many communities move into Baptism by immersion simply because they realize that the reality of conversion is so powerful that a few drops of water cannot adequately express what is going on in the elect or in the life of the community that initiates them.

The Scriptures and prayers of the Easter Vigil are eloquent about the mystery of water and its role in redemption. The central Old Testament passage, which must always be read, is the crossing of the Red Sea. Large quantities of water, indeed walls of water and water as an occasion of life and death, set the tone. When we bless the water of the font, we remember Noah and the flood, and the Baptism of Jesus in the Jordan river. According to Scripture scholars, the Vigil reading from Romans, like many other passages from the Pauline letters, presumes the practice of Baptism by immersion and reflects upon it, using imagery of death, burial, and resurrection. To somehow suggest that the waters of Baptism are an occasion of death and new life, an adequate quantity of water must be used. (It has been noted that "no one has ever been sprinkled to death.") The Scriptures and prayers of the Vigil, therefore, also invite us to a generous use of water so that we can make the connections between Baptism and the events of saving history.

Preparing the Team

If your parish is contemplating the move to Baptism by immersion, the following may be helpful:

- ✧ Share the theological and pastoral reasons for Baptism by immersion.

- ✧ Read RCIA 6, 18–20, 22, 213, 226A, National Statutes 17.

- ✧ Find a community similar to yours that has implemented Baptism by immersion, and invite their catechumenate director to describe how and why they did it.

- ✧ Invite someone who has experienced Baptism by immersion to tell about their experience.

- ✧ View the video "This Is the Night" (LTP).

A discussion of practical elements, such as those that follow, would then be helpful.

Constructing a Temporary Immersion Font

Any large, watertight container can be the basis for a temporary immersion font. A frame of stone or wood or brick can be built around the outside of the container to make a beautiful and noble exterior for what may be utilitarian and plain underneath (such as a farm trough or a pool obtained from a landscape supply company). Natural materials that reflect the environment of your community and that combine well with the interior of your church are desirable. Two kinds of basins are possible: those that hold enough water for the elect to go down into it and be immersed, and those which serve as a catch basin for water that is poured from large pitchers or jugs over the elect, drenching them completely.

Ideally, the font would be large enough to accommodate both the person being baptized and the minister of Baptism. Steps are usually needed to get in and out of the font. Because those who have been baptized will emerge from the font soaking wet, it is helpful to have an absorbent rug on the floor nearby the place where they exit from the font, where they can stand until they receive their garments and candles and go to a room where they will change into dry clothes.

Preparing the Elect and Their Godparents

All through the process of initiation, those who are being initiated do not rehearse. Their sponsors rehearse, and the catechumens and candidates prepare spiritually. The Easter Vigil is no exception. Nonetheless, the elect must be prepared in some specific practical ways for Baptism by immersion. They need to be told that they will get completely wet. Here are some items to share with them.

- ✧ They should come dressed in clothes which they don't mind getting wet. (Some parishes supply robes to be worn into the font over whatever the elect are wearing. Such robes should be of a contrasting color to the garment that is given to them after Baptism.)

- ✧ Whatever they wear on their feet should be easy to take on and off.

- ✧ They should not spend money and effort on an elaborate hairdo.

If the anointing for Confirmation will use a generous amount of oil, they also need to be told this.

The godparents need to be prepared to be of practical assistance to the elect, first of all by helping them into the font. After Baptism, they assist with towels, and with the presentation of a baptismal garment and lighted candle. They accompany them to another room with them and help them change into dry clothes. In order to keep an atmosphere of prayer, one of the godparents could read aloud again the reading from Romans or some other suitable text as the newly baptized are changing their clothes. They then accompany the neophytes back into the assembly for Confirmation.

Preparing the Rite

When using the combined rite, both the renewal of Baptism by the assembly and the "Rite of Reception" take place while the newly baptized are changing into dry clothes. If you do not plan to use the combined rite, it would still be a good idea to renew the baptismal commitment of the assembly at this time, so that when the newly baptized return to the assembly, they can move directly into the celebration of Confirmation. The time needed for the neophytes to get changed may not be very long, but in order to maintain some flexibility in the ritual, the music ministry should be prepared to lead the assembly in song while waiting for the neophytes to rejoin them.

What About Chrism?

Be sure to obtain from your diocese an adequate amount of sacred chrism, so that the anointing of Confirmation comes up to the standards set by the full use of the symbol of water. Unlike the other oils, which are blessed, chrism is consecrated by the bishop at the Chrism Mass and may not be augmented by other oils. Remember that the quantity is judged adequate by how much of it you actually use. Large quantities for display purposes, as a visual symbol, are not appropriate; but if you intend to actually use a considerable amount for the anointing, most diocesan offices are happy to provide whatever you need.